SURVIVAL

Childlike Faith Series

PHILIP HAHN

© 2017 Philip Hahn
Published by SourceBox Productions
P.O. Box 231241 Tigard, OR 97281
www.sourceboxproductions.com

Printed in the United States of America

Cover by Jesh Designs
Edited by Blake Atwood

All rights reserved. No part of this publication may be reproduced, stored in a retrieval system, or transmitted in any form or by any means—for example, electronic, photocopy, recording—without the prior written permission of the publisher. The only exception is brief quotations in printed reviews.
ISBN-10: 0-9987927-0-5
ISBN-13: 978-0-9987927-0-5

All scripture is taken from the New International Version unless otherwise noted.

TO ARNIE & BARB BURLEY

from whom came more powerful affirmation and encouragement than they realize. It is because of people like you this book was written.

CONTENTS

Introduction

Chapter 1: Survival

Chapter 2: We Need Water

Chapter 3: We Need Food

Chapter 4: We Need Fire

Chapter 5: We Need Shelter

Chapter 6: Make It Real

INTRODUCTION

Okay, you picked up this book and you'd like to get right into the nitty gritty of the content. But I've learned that you should never trust information unless you know its source. Heaven help us if we blindly believe everything we read or hear. So please always ask the question, "Why should I believe this?" about everything you read and measure it against the truth of God's Word.

So who am I? My name is Philip Hahn. I grew up in a pastor's home. My dad was the children's pastor at the same church in Joliet, Illinois for twenty-six years. I had a puppet in my hand and a hymn in my mouth before I hit kindergarten. But more importantly than that, I genuinely surrendered my life to serve Jesus at age four. It was the real deal. I didn't have to understand the theology of substitutionary atonement. I didn't have to go to a class. The only thing I understood was that I had sinned and separated myself from God, but Jesus loved me and wanted to help me live better than that. If you're wondering what Christianity is really about, that's it. We're wrong; God's right, so live for Jesus.

I felt a calling into full-time ministry at age seven and have been working to teach others about God ever since. I grew up, went off to Bible College in Minnesota, got a Bachelor's Degree in Children's Pastoral Ministry, met my wife, and moved back to the Chicago area. I spent the next thirteen years as a children's pastor in Illinois, Michigan, and Oregon. I led evangelism teams at camps, crusades, and outreaches teaching kids all over the United States.

The years I spent living in the home of a Children's Pastor, my education in Bible College, and my experience professionally teaching kids convinced me of something profound: any scriptural truth can be taught to a kindergartener if taught simply. Christianity isn't complicated. So, in my ministry, I never held back the whole truth and meaning of any part of the Bible from the kids.

But there was a side effect I didn't anticipate. As parents, volunteers, and other adults observed or attended my children's classes, I was astonished at how many of them told me they found the teaching amazing. Don't get me wrong; they weren't impressed with me. They were impressed with the content. They expressed how simple it was. They told me that I should record the classes or teach the adults this stuff. A lot of the basic things I was teaching the kids were things the adults had never learned, or at least never fully understood.

Slowly, I was given more and more opportunities to preach and teach to adults. Each time they expressed their amazement at how simple the message was but also at how profound the truth was. The real wake-up call for me was when I was given the opportunity to teach a five-week series to a large adult Sunday School class. This class consisted of thirty to forty-five adults, some of whom had only been attending for a short time, while others had been strong Christians who had attended for decades. For five weeks, I spoke about the basic habits every Christian needs in their life. Basically, read your Bible and pray.

I didn't know if any of this would be relevant to a sixty-year-old who had been a Christian longer than I'd been alive. But once again, I received an overwhelming response from both new Christians and experienced Christians about how inspirational and enlightening the content was. I was telling church board members why they needed to read their Bible and they were thanking me. These were not ignorant people; they were mature, well-grounded, healthy believers. In every definition of the word, they were good Christians. But still they were expressing their regret that I hadn't recorded my teaching.

Then my wife suggested that I write a few books similar to the class I'd taught. She thought a lot of adults, teens, and kids could benefit from a very simple explanation of the basics of biblical faith. You hold in your hand the result of that suggestion. I finally recorded it.

Sometimes we need to be reminded of what is truly important. Sometimes we still don't understand the why of what we believe. Sometimes we never received the foundational concepts that we should have started with. So, from my education and experience, here are a few things I think you might find helpful.

CHAPTER 1: SURVIVAL

WHY?

You won't receive any tools in this chapter. Imagine being handed an unidentified pill and being told to swallow it without any further explanation. That's ridiculous. You wouldn't swallow some mysterious pill without knowing a few things first. You might even get angry at whoever offered it to you. You would want to know exactly what it was and why you should take it before you swallowed it, wouldn't you? You would never accept medicine until you were convinced you needed it. You have to understand the *why* before you'll accept the *what*.

Most of us also know our own human natures. There are some things we think we already know, and it's hard to hear someone tell us something we already know. If a person is unhealthy, chances are good that he probably knows the solution is diet and exercise, but even if he's not dieting and exercising, it's really hard to listen to advice to diet and exercise. Without a wake-up call that motivates us or the required knowledge to act, we will never act to change our lifestyles.

Over the next few chapters, I will be talking about things that may feel like I'm saying, "Diet and exercise." Without this chapter's *why* foundation, it would be too easy to simply think, "Duh, I knew that," even though we might not be doing it.

SECTION 1: WHY SURVIVAL?

A natural first question could be why I chose to frame these essentials for life into a "survival" theme. First of all, it's not a macho thing. Despite traditional stereotypes, men are not the only providers and protectors. There's an ingrained instinct to survive in every living creature. From the single-celled organism to the smartest primates, animals react when they perceive a threat to survival. It's the fight or flight response. People, however, can take it a step further. We can prepare to survive *before* we feel threatened. This advantage has placed us on top of the food chain, and I believe it to be one of many characteristics we've inherited from God that separates us from the animals.

The primary reason I put this series into the context of a survival kit is that there are some basic spiritual habits, or disciplines, that a Christian simply cannot live without, though many Christians have tried. Remove any of these habits from your life and you risk total failure of your faith with eternal consequences. You can name any spiritual need, theology, moral issue, or life problem and all of them will boil down to one of four essential spiritual disciplines which will be described in the following chapters. In other words, with all the survival essentials in proper balance, you will survive. With any one of them missing, you may not.

Let me be clear though. These are not salvation issues; they are survival issues. When a person is given life at birth, they didn't have to do anything to obtain life, but there will be many essentials they will have to fulfill in order to retain that life in a healthy manner.

Likewise, for the Christian believer who has been born again and started a new life following Jesus, they didn't have to do anything to obtain the forgiveness of their sins, but there are some essentials they will need in order to continue living that life in a growing and healthy way. If they don't have these essentials, they risk losing any abundant life Christianity has to offer. Without intentional effort, you jeopardize losing all the hope, faith, power, and help that you initially gained by following Jesus. You may even reach a point where you wonder why you're a Christian at all. You may technically be saved, but miserably unhealthy. That's why we need to be intentional about survival.

Think for just a moment about why people train and educate themselves to survive in the wild. Why would someone want to learn to sustain himself without a microwave, running water, and a roof over his head? No, really, stop reading and try to come up with three reasons why a person might study survival skills.

I'll wait.

I bet at least one of your answers started out with the words, "Just in case." Have there ever been any what-if scenarios that you've worried about or have prepared for? Think about it. Men, why do you carry a pen or a pocketknife in your jeans? Women, why do you carry tissues or lip balm in your purse? You believe there are a few things you might need but won't have available when you step away from your home or office. We all prepare on some level. Some even take it to extremes, planning for what they would do if a disaster struck and they were forced to live completely self-sufficiently.

I put survivalists into three categories. The first are those I call Boy Scout-ready. They are prepared with basic knowledge and/or supplies if the things they depend on are not available for some reason. They know where the flashlight is if the power goes out or how to find north by identifying the North Star in the night sky.

The second group of survivalists is the doomsday preppers. They train, practice, and stock provisions on a regular basis with the expectation that something will go wrong. They must always be prepared to live off of nothing but their own efforts for an extended period of time. These are the people who have bombproof bunkers well stocked with supplies and knowledge on how to gather food in the wild.

The third group is those who fall somewhere between those two extremes. At some level, I think we all prepare for the unknown. Where do you think you fall on this scale? How often do you think of or prepare for the unexpected?

I am a bit of a casual survival enthusiast, but I'm not a fanatic. I have assembled a few small survival kits for when I go camping, and I keep quite a few little supplies stuffed into my computer bag in case I need them. But I'm nothing compared to some people I have seen on television. I have seen shows that detail peoples' preparations for nuclear war, economic collapse, viral pandemics, and natural disasters. I saw an episode where a woman not only packed her storage rooms with emergency food supplies, but also stuffed them into her ceiling, her mattress, and even the inside of her hollow doors. People in these shows go to extreme preparation levels because they are convinced of the certainty of disaster and dedicate their lives to being ready for it.

Regardless of what they are preparing for, I have observed one thing in common between all the people I've watched on these television shows: fear. Each one is afraid of the what-if. What if disaster strikes or society collapses? Will I be prepared? Will I be able to provide for my family? Their response to that fear is extreme preparation for all possible threats.

Now, before I go into assembling our survival kit, I want to make one thing clear. We have *nothing* to fear if society collapses or disaster strikes. We are citizens of another kingdom. The worst thing that can happen is death. You can't scare me with the threat of heaven. There's nothing to fear in the physical realm. But in the spiritual realm, eternity is at stake and God has provided for our survival.

As Luke said, "I tell you, my friends, do not be afraid of those who kill the body and after that can do no more. But I will show you whom you should fear: Fear him who, after your body has been killed, has authority to throw you into hell. Yes, I tell you, fear him. Are not five sparrows sold for two pennies? Yet not one of them is forgotten by God. Indeed, the very hairs of your head are all numbered. Don't be afraid; you are worth more than many sparrows" (Luke 12:4–7).

And as Paul reminded us in Philippians 4:6–7, "Do not be anxious about anything, but in every situation, by prayer and petition, with thanksgiving, present your requests to God. And the peace of God, which transcends all understanding, will guard your hearts and your minds in Christ Jesus."

SECTION 2: FROM IF TO WHEN

There may be nothing to fear in the physical realm, but eternity is a very long time, and we should really be focused on what our condition will be when entering into that eternity.

First, tear down the illusion that you are safe and secure. Some people worry about the "if" question. They wonder what would happen "if" something bad happens. But when there is an actual disaster, they move quickly into the "when" camp. When something bad happens they are convinced that they should have been prepared. The situation moves very quickly from "if" to "when" after it's too late. Spiritually, you have to see that it's too late. We are already in a survival situation and we don't even know it. There's already an enemy who's already hunting you.

The apostle Peter reminded believers to,

> *Humble yourselves,* therefore, under God's mighty hand, that he may lift you up in due time. Cast all your anxiety on him because he cares for you. *Be alert and of sober mind.* Your enemy the *devil prowls around like a roaring lion looking for someone to devour.* Resist him, standing firm in the faith, because you know that the family of believers throughout the world is undergoing the *same kind of*

sufferings. And the God of all grace, who called you to his eternal glory in Christ, after you have *suffered a little while*, will himself restore you and make you strong, firm and steadfast (1 Peter 5:7–10, emphasis added).

We don't live in fear, but we're not safe.

Second, because physical needs are already met in your home, you feel safe when you really are not. This illusion of safety is like carbon monoxide, a dangerous chemical not only because it can kill you, but because of *how* it kills you. Carbon monoxide is an odorless, tasteless, colorless gas. When you breathe it, your body actually accepts it as if it is oxygen. Your lungs pull it in and send it straight to the blood your heart pumps throughout your system. The poison kills you before you realize its presence.

Physical comfort is like carbon monoxide. When you feel comfortable you cannot detect the spiritual needs that may be killing you. It's a placebo that lies to your system, telling you that everything is fine when, in reality, everything is not fine. How do you fight an enemy you cannot see? How do you prepare for a threat you don't feel looming over you?

We don't live in fear, but we're not safe.

I don't know where you fall on the survivalist scale, but whether you're a Boy Scout or a doomsday prepper, can you see the need for Christians to be spiritual doomsday preppers? We are already under attack, but most of us are not acting like it.

Third, you're never ready. Some believe they are mature Christians, and many are. Others believe they are inadequate and have a long way to go, and that might be true. But everyone who is honest with themselves will admit that room for improvement exists. The problem is that very few are taking action to improve themselves.

I have a folder in my filing cabinet that is about six inches thick (so far) full of various teaching materials, notes, classes, and information I have gathered over the years to help me become a better leader, pastor, and follower of Jesus. I call it my self-improvement folder. Do you think I have everything in that folder mastered? Of course not. So why do I keep trying to improve myself?

The word "entropy" refers to the inevitable decay everything suffers. Naturally, everything is subject to entropy. Everything breaks down eventually. The hardest rock is slowly worn away by the flow of water, wind, and weather. The most powerful governments and kingdoms of the world all eventually fail and collapse. Every individual has areas where their life is in decline, not growth.

Entropy is a lot like gravity. Gravity is an irresistible force. You cannot cancel gravity. You can temporarily overcome gravity by jumping up in the air, but it will still pull you back down. You can counteract gravity by using an engine and a few wings to lift you off the ground and fly for long periods of time, but the engine can't run forever. Eventually, it has to come back down to the ground. Even a rocket that propels people into space will only keep them out there until their supplies run out. Then they either have to return to the gravity of the earth or die.

No matter how ready we are, the gravitational pull of entropy will bring us back to a place where we are not as ready as we used to be. It seems as if we can only keep up the pace of being prepared as long as we feel the need, and comfort makes sure we don't feel the need very long. Then, just as soon as we think we're ready, the threats and challenges change and we are suddenly right back where we started.

In high school, I was in the Junior Reserve Officers' Training Corps (JROTC), an educational version of the army where young people learn to function as if they were in the military. For some, it leads to serious careers in the armed forces. While there I learned the difference between ready and prepared.

When we would put on our uniforms and line up for inspection, the inspecting officer would go over every aspect of our dress and demeanor to determine if we were keeping up with their standard of expectation. We were supposed to have our uniforms clean and in proper order. Our shirts and belts were supposed to be aligned. Our brass insignia and shoes were supposed to be polished. Our posture was supposed to reflect the position in which we were commanded to stand.

When we would line up, we were expected to say, "Prepared for inspection, Sergeant!" We learned very fast never to say, "Ready for inspection, Sergeant!" Prepared meant that I had organized and arranged myself to the best of my ability to meet whatever standard was expected of me. Ready meant that I had missed nothing; I had everything perfect. If we thought we were *ready* for inspection, it became the Sergeant's personal mission to point out everything he could find that was *not* perfect with us.

Listen. We are *never* ready. We never have everything perfect. We will never arrive at knowing everything we need to know in order to meet every spiritual challenge life has to offer. We can only be prepared. We can only line up and say, "I'm doing as much as I know how in this moment to prepare myself for what is coming my way, and I'll continue preparing because I know I'll never be ready."

But that's a good thing. Knowing you're never ready relieves the pressure. You don't have to be perfect. You just have to continue preparing. Even if you fail, you can still prepare for your next challenge. This continual preparation also prevents you from getting arrogant enough to think you're ready. The moment you think you're ready, the Devil will look you up and down and find the one weak spot you didn't think about. When you know you're never ready, it keeps you inspired to always prepare. The point is that you never stop preparing.

SECTION 3: THE PROBLEM ISN'T

Now we come to the problem. You know what your problem is? You have problems. Everyone has them, and everyone will continue to have them for the rest of their lives. But the truth is, your problem might not have anything to do with your problems.

Based on my understanding of Scripture and my experience in life, I believe that all problems stem from, or are cured by, our connection with God. You don't have a problem with pornography; you are seeking satisfaction in an area that is supposed to be satisfied with the presence of God. You don't have a problem with anger; you have a lack of the spiritual fruit of peace. You don't need less anger; you need more Spirit. You don't have a problem with an unreasonable boss, but you might have a problem with finding God's joy, love, and contentment despite the circumstances.

You don't have a problem with your problem; it's just a symptom of your lack of Jesus in that area. Let me stop here and be very clear: this does *not* mean that believers have no problems. Rain falls on the righteous and the wicked, but the righteous get an umbrella. What I'm saying is that if you have a proper connection with Jesus, the problems can be overcome.

When we face a challenge, focusing on the problem is like complaining about the symptoms without looking at the disease. You can sit in your bed miserably complaining about your sinus congestion and your cough and your sore throat. Then you can reach for medicine that numbs or temporarily relieves those uncomfortable symptoms. Then the medicine wears off and you're still stuck with the disease that's causing all these symptoms.

We focus on the problems with people in our lives, the circumstances we are forced to live in, and the events that take place around us. These are the things that make us uncomfortable. These are the felt needs we think are the problems. These are the sore throats and stuffy noses that make us reach for medicine like counselors, self-help books, and even our own reasoning.

Now, there's nothing wrong with these treatments. I take Nyquil when I get a cold to treat the symptoms. I have been to counselors, I am writing a self-help book, and without our own reasoning we would never be able to survive. But I *also* want to treat the disease causing the symptoms. I want to cure my cold. I want to take vitamin C, get more sleep, wash my hands, and pray for healing because I know that numbing the symptoms is only a part of the battle. Getting rid of the disease is the real end goal that wins the war and ends the symptoms altogether.

So don't worry about the discomfort of your situation until you meet your basic needs. Survival is not about feeling comfortable; it is about living to see tomorrow. And you don't live to see tomorrow if your first instinct is to address your comfort level. Push past the discomfort and meet your basic needs, and then you can worry about how you feel.

Essentially, if we don't prepare to survive by meeting our most basic needs first, nothing else matters. It doesn't matter how comfortable your shelter is if you died three days ago from dehydration. It doesn't matter how perfect your construction above ground may be if it is not built on a firm foundation. It doesn't matter whether your career or relationships are falling apart if your personal spiritual habits are out of alignment. The reason your life is falling over might not be because the walls are broken. You may need to build a foundation with Jesus first before you even start talking about the walls of careers or relationships. If we don't get the basics right, all other areas of our life suffer. But if we do get the basics right, all other areas of our life flourish.

SECTION 4: THE SURVIVAL MINDSET

Before you even think about survival in any capacity, you need the survival mindset. In the survivalist television shows I referred to earlier, one of the key components the experts used to gauge how prepared someone was to meet a challenge was the "Survival Mindset." This referred to the warrior's force of will to overcome the problem at hand and muscle through, doing whatever it took to live.

When in an actual survival situation, all experts say morale is vital, but few people take such advice seriously until placed in a life-threatening situation. Being placed in a situation where you might not live to see tomorrow is extremely demoralizing. That is one of the reasons keeping your spirits up is so important. People with the equipment, training, and know-how to survive in the wild have simply laid down and died because they perceived their situations to be hopeless. Then there were others who, in spite of severe injury and overwhelming obstacles, pushed themselves beyond their limits and made it out alive.

The warm crackle of a fire can be a very comforting and hopeful inspiration to someone who is cold and lonely. Some recommend placing photographs of loved ones in your survival kit so you know why you have to live and who you're fighting for. Your focus determines your reality. The survival mindset takes your focus off of your immediate problem or discomfort and places it on the more important need at hand. Then, instead of wallowing in your own self-pity, you can get on your feet and do something about it.

For a Christian, the single biggest paradigm shift in life is when we realize that it's all about God and not us. Many may believe that God is in charge, but if you ask them to let God decide what movies they watch, what friends they hang out with, or whether they should drink alcohol, they'll protest the statement as a violation of their rights. The truth is, I have no rights.

I deserve the consequences my crimes have brought on me. Every day that God chooses *not* to deal out the punishment my sins deserve is a miracle of grace. In addition to that freedom, all of the undeserved blessing he continues to pour out on me despite what I truly deserve is just as miraculous. As our Creator, he already deserves every part of our lives. But as our Savior and Redeemer, we owe him more than we could ever repay. You have no rights to anything other than punishment. If God says jump off a cliff—he's not going to say that, by the way—your response should be to Google the nearest cliff and start running toward it.

If God is *truly* in charge, it doesn't matter how secure we *feel.* When God says the following chapters are essential things we need for our survival, we don't try to argue our way out of them. We don't rationalize our rights and say, "That's a good idea, but I'm getting along fine without it." When God commands, we obey. If we don't, we die. Eternity is a long time. Don't risk your eternity trying to come up with your own way to follow God.

Before we assemble a spiritual survival kit over the next four chapters, you need to get the survival mindset that predetermines you are going to win no matter what it takes. You are not going to let comfort, discomfort, distractions, or actions keep you from doing things the way *God* wants. Admit ahead of time that he's smarter than you are. Do it his way and you will not only survive, you'll thrive.

SECTION 5: MY EXPERIENCE

As a pastor, I can tell you it is quite easy to go through the motions. Temptations are always around, picking away at your willpower. Spiritual entropy and apathy affect spiritual leaders just as much as everyone else. The problem as a ministry leader though, is that the proximity to the things of God gave me the illusion of intimacy of God. I don't believe there was ever a time in my life where I backslid and jeopardized my salvation. But there were plenty of times where I experienced so little power, satisfaction, or divine impact in my life. I needed to connect with God in the intimate way that hanging around church can never provide. I needed to make it personal.

When I was pastoring in Michigan, an evangelist named Dean came to our church. His ministry had demonstrated amazing success. His ministries had seen thousands saved, and miracles, signs, and wonders abounded. He was passionately in love with Jesus and his enthusiasm overflowed into every area of his life. Everywhere Dean went, the love of Jesus emanated from him and influenced everyone around him.

When people asked him the secret as to why his ministry had experienced so much power, impact, and success, Dean said he prayed in tongues and read his Bible, each for at least an hour a day. No one believed his success was due to something so simple. They kept trying to prod him into telling them strategies and techniques and leadership secrets, but his answer was just an hour of Bible reading and an hour of prayer. So he challenged everyone in the room to just try it for two weeks and see what happens.

For one week I read my Bible for an hour a day and prayed for an hour a day. It was the most powerful week of my life. I felt so full of God's presence and purpose. Creativity, joy, satisfaction, and peace flowed abundantly. I felt like a new man. So why didn't I continue this pattern for the second week?

Gravity.

No matter how strong my leap, gravity and entropy eventually pulled me back down. I couldn't keep up with that pace. I got distracted. I wanted to sleep in. I had no one to hold me accountable to the new pattern. Pick whatever excuse you want. I didn't stick with it despite the fact that I knew how awesome that Bible reading and prayer time was and what it could do in my life.

It's not enough to break free for a moment; you have to constantly keep up with gravity. That's why we have to prepare for survival, because the threats are always changing.

Here's how recent this struggle is for me. Five months prior to writing this book, I started waking up at 6:00 a.m. to pray. I'm not a morning person. I never get up that early unless I have to. I prefer waking up at eight or maybe ten on my day off. But that was the only time I had that I knew wouldn't be interrupted by kids, work, or other distractions. It continues to be harder for my flesh to keep up that pace. But it also continues to be more beneficial for my spirit. I had to partner with a friend who could commit to the same schedule in order to hold myself accountable to keep up the pace. It is hard work to train for survival, but I will die without Jesus.

WHAT'S NEXT?

Ask yourself these four questions: No, really. Stop and answer each one.

1. Does the enemy of my soul ever quit?
2. On my own, can I ever predict all potential threats?
3. Does God have what it takes to help me?
4. Do I still need to learn how to prepare?

If you are convinced that you need to sharpen your spiritual survival skills, then commit now before reading any further that there are areas in your life where you are vulnerable. Decide for yourself that you must and will continue preparing yourself for the ever-changing challenges for the rest of your life. Don't get overwhelmed though; it's not as hard as you might think.

You only need four things in your survival kit, but the items expire and you will need to replenish them regularly. If you are ready, read on and commit to a deeper pursuit of Christ than your current lifestyle.

CHAPTER 2: WE NEED WATER

PRAYER

Before reading this next chapter, it's not only fitting but absolutely necessary to pray. Read this prayer and direct your words to God. Think about them and don't read any further until you can mean every word: "God, my heart is open. My spirit is ready. Get inside me. You have my permission to change me from the inside. Speak; your servant is listening."

Let's quickly review the last chapter:

1. Tear down the illusion that you're safe and secure.
2. You're already in a survival situation. (The Devil is a roaring lion and an active, ongoing threat).
3. Comfort lies to you like a placebo or carbon monoxide. It tricks you into thinking you're okay.
4. See the need to become a spiritual doomsday prepper.

5. You're never ready. The threats keep changing, so you need to continually prepare.

With the following questions, be honest with yourself and think about what you really do from day to day. There's no reason to feel bad or good about your answers. This is just the starting point. Before you determine where you're going, you have to determine where you are.

1. How many days this week did you spend intimate time alone with Jesus in prayer? Do you think this was enough time? Why or why not?
2. On average, how long do you spend in prayer in a single day? Do you think this is enough time? Why or why not?

SECTION 1: THE NEED FOR WATER

According to livestrong.com you can last three to seven days without water. If you're already healthy, well-hydrated, and placed in an ideal controlled environment, you could theoretically make it seven days before you died. But more likely, if you're outdoors in a survival situation, hot weather, disease, initial poor hydration, exertion, as well as any number of adverse conditions will kill you from dehydration in three days.

But even on the first day without water, your body already starts the process of dying. Dehydration is one of the most dangerous and painful things you can do to your body.

Prayer is water. Why parallel prayer with water? It's the most important thing in the universe. Abraham and Moses didn't have Bibles or churches. They only had one thing: their own personal communication with God. If you can get this right, God can directly help you figure out the rest. It might be harder without anything else to help you, but your personal communication with God in prayer technically contains everything necessary for your survival. If your prayer and personal connection with God are strong enough, he can personally communicate to you everything you need.

But many people get the wrong idea about prayer. Prayer is not asking God for things. God is not a giant Santa Claus in the sky who brings you everything on your wish list. He is not a magic genie here to grant your three wishes. Prayer is not something you do; it's who you are.

There are many definitions of prayer that may be more complete than what I share with you here. But for the purpose of this chapter, I'm defining prayer as **spending intimate time communicating with God.**

The Bible feeds us knowledge and understanding. Worship expresses our love and submission. (We'll discuss Bible study and worship in a later chapter.) But prayer provides intimate communication. Without this personal and intimate communication channel, nothing else can flow. Worship would become impersonal, Bible-reading would become mechanical, and church would become an obligation.

SECTION 2: IT'S RELATIONAL, NOT RELIGIOUS.

In 1 Thessalonians 5:17, Paul simply reminds us, "Pray continually." Does that mean we should crawl through life on our knees with our heads bowed or order food at the drive-through window with our eyes closed? Of course not.

How do you communicate to your closest family and friends? Do you lock eye contact with them in a never-ending stream of words? Of course not. When you're walking down the street with your family or hanging out with your friends at the mall, you're just bouncing conversation back and forth about your day. Then there are periods where no one feels the need to say anything. But when you see something worth mentioning, or think about a subject that someone else might find interesting, you just mention it because they're right there walking beside you. And if they have something to say, you're right there to listen.

What do you talk about with your family and friends? Are your conversations only consumed with what you want them to do for you? I hope not. That would be an unhealthy relationship.

Think again for a moment about your closest friend or family member.

Are you close because you communicate or do you communicate because you're close?

If you're close because you communicate, the moment you drop out of communication, intimacy disappears. If you communicate because you're close, then a lack of communication would indicate you're not close anymore. One is a cause, the other an effect, but either way, without communication there is no intimacy.

"Pray continually" means that you walk through life with Jesus at your side. You walk where he goes and he walks where you go. When there's something you feel is worth bringing up, he's the one you bring it up to. When he has something to say, you're right there to listen.

It's not religious, it's relational.

SECTION 3: LIVING WATER

The following story about Jesus from the book of John is so integral to our understanding of prayer that we need to read it in its entirety:

> So he [Jesus] left Judea and returned to Galilee.
>
> He had to go through Samaria on the way. Eventually he came to the Samaritan village of Sychar, near the field that Jacob gave to his son Joseph. Jacob's well was there; and Jesus, tired from the long walk, sat wearily beside the well about noontime. Soon a Samaritan woman came to draw water, and Jesus said to her, "Please give me a drink." He was alone at the time because his disciples had gone into the village to buy some food.
>
> The woman was surprised, for Jews refuse to have anything to do with Samaritans. She said to Jesus, "You are a Jew, and I am a Samaritan woman. Why are you asking me for a drink?"
>
> Jesus replied, *"If you only knew the gift God has for you and who you are speak-*

ing to, you would ask me, and I would give you living water."

"But sir, you don't have a rope or a bucket," she said, "and this well is very deep. Where would you get this living water? And besides, do you think you're greater than our ancestor Jacob, who gave us this well? How can you offer better water than he and his sons and his animals enjoyed?"

Jesus replied, "Anyone who drinks this water will soon become thirsty again. But those who drink the water I give will never be thirsty again. It becomes a fresh, bubbling spring within them, giving them eternal life."

"Please, sir," the woman said, "give me this water! Then I'll never be thirsty again, and I won't have to come here to get water."

"Go and get your husband," Jesus told her.

"I don't have a husband," the woman replied.

Jesus said, "You're right! You don't have a husband—for you have had five hus-

> bands, and you aren't even married to the man you're living with now. You certainly spoke the truth! (John 4:3–18, NLT, emphasis added)

Let's unpack this. This woman came for one thing: water. She was a Samaritan. It's obvious from the text that Jews didn't associate with Samaritans. They were half-breeds, social outcasts considered to be unclean, immoral, bad influences on decent society. Regardless of whether this opinion of Samaritans was justified, the point is that Jesus didn't care. He wanted to bring something more than just water to this woman to temporarily fulfill her physical needs. I believe he wants to bring more to you too. He wants to bring you the same living water he offered her.

"If you only knew the *gift* God has for you."

Reader, if you only knew the gift God has for you in this intimate relationship he's offering. If you only knew the *abundance* of this gift. If you only knew how *satisfying* this gift is. If you only knew how this gift of intimacy would change your life, you wouldn't be able to run to Jesus fast enough to get it.

"If you only knew . . . *who* you are speaking to."

Reader, if you only knew the one you're speaking to. If you only knew the full extent of his power. If you only knew how deeply and unconditionally *he loves you*. If you only knew how a relationship with Jesus would personally, intimately, and deeply change your life forever, you wouldn't be able to run to him fast enough.

"If you only knew . . . you would *ask* me."

Reader, if you had even the slightest understanding of who Jesus is and what he's capable of giving you, you would never cease in asking him what he has to offer, what he wants for your life, or what new, amazing, and extraordinary gift he has in store for you next. You would be asking and asking and asking at every opportunity because you would know that he's the only one capable of delivering every time. He might not deliver the water you were expecting, but in every way possible he will deliver the water you need.

"Anyone who drinks *this* water will soon become thirsty again. But those who drink the water *I give* will never be thirsty again. It becomes a fresh, bubbling spring within them, giving them *eternal* life."

Friend, when you seek for what you think you need, you will always have to go back for more, because what you think you need will always leave you thirsty again. When you seek first the *Giver,* his *living* water satisfies your soul in ways you never would have thought to ask for.

"You don't have a husband—for you have had five husbands, and you aren't even married to the man you're living with now."

Ouch! Wait, that doesn't sound like living water. When I get into an intimate conversation with Jesus, will he start pointing out all my flaws?

Jesus loves you. Jesus knows you. He knows every hair on your head, every tear you've cried, and yes, every mistake you've made. But the point was that Jesus knew this woman was a Samaritan, an adulterer, and a very wicked, unapologetic sinner. The point was that Jesus wanted to talk to her anyway!

We're not fooling anyone, especially God. We're all sinners. But who, other than Jesus, would know our every evil thought and *still* want to give us his living water? No one knows you better than he does, and no one cares more deeply for you. *That's* a conversation worth having. He accepts you with all your sin, but loves you too much to let you continue suffering in it.

That's living water.

SECTION 4: STAY CONNECTED

I wonder how smart you are. I bet you know enough about plants to tell the difference between a living branch and a dead branch, but just to make sure, let's test your knowledge.

You hold in your hands two branches, one living and one dead. On the left you hold a branch that remained connected to the trunk of a tree until only moments ago. On the right you hold a branch that has been disconnected from the trunk for several months.

Can you tell which is which?

Now, before you finalize your answer about which branch is alive and which is dead, remember that a true scientist collects all the data before coming to a conclusion. There are two more clues ahead. Please hold off on making your choice until the end of the test.

The branch in your left hand received a regular flow of water and nutrients that passed up from the soil to the roots and through the trunk. The branch in your right hand has had no moisture or nutrients in a long time. It hasn't had access to anything the soil, roots, or trunk had to offer.

I know you think you know the answer at this point, but I've left out a crucial clue that will inform you which branch is living and which is dead. The branch in your left hand is soft and pliable. It bends and flexes under stress and is difficult to break. The branch in your right hand is dry and brittle. It cracks under stress and is easy to break.

I hope you found that little exercise a bit ridiculous. It should be painfully obvious which branch is living and which is dead. The signs are so apparent; it seems silly to even pose the question. But, as an author and public speaker, I wouldn't make you admit to an easily obvious truth without dropping the question that brings the illustration home: which branch are you?

You may believe you're connected to the trunk, but let's test that with some scientific observations:

1. How much time did you spend talking with Jesus today in prayer?
2. How much time did you spend with Jesus yesterday?
3. Is he a part of all your decisions?
4. In how much of your life did you totally include Jesus this week?

Recall John 15:5: "I am the vine; you are the branches. If you remain in me and I in you, you will bear much fruit; apart from me you can do nothing."

What can you do without staying connected to Jesus? Nothing! The only personal connection you have to Jesus is your daily interactions with him in prayer. Where else do you have the opportunity to stay connected in a give-and-take flow where you both share with him and receive from him? All the effort and knowledge you can muster will amount to nothing unless you stay connected to the vine. How would you feel if you spent a lifetime trying your hardest to make things succeed only to find out they were always doomed to fail?

Thirty seconds of prayer before your meals, or a sixty-second wish list before you go to bed, is not staying connected to Jesus. It does a branch no good to simply touch the trunk every once in a while. A branch must be physically attached and inseparable from the trunk in order to have access to the moisture and nutrients the trunk has to offer. Could any branch produce fruit if it spent any significant time separated from the trunk? The true nature of prayer is that there is never a part of your life that is not connected in conversation to God.

On a personal note, I don't pretend to have this perfect in my own life. Remember, as a component in an ever-replenishing survival kit, no one has ever arrived at being perfect. But staying increasingly connected to Jesus in prayer is essential to keeping our survival kits stocked with the fresh supply of water and nutrients our souls require.

Apart from him we can do nothing.

SECTION 5: MUSCLE MEMORY

Don't wait until you need help before you decide your response. Prayer allows you to practice connecting with Jesus *before* you need him, so when you really need him you're already connected. You don't have to go looking for his power.

If you're often tempted to steal, standing in the department store next to a desired item you can't afford is not the right time to decide how you'll respond. There are many examples of how this concept plays out in real life.

For most of my life, I've been studying martial arts, primarily karate and jujitsu. One of the primary reasons most people study martial arts is for self-defense. If untrained and unprepared individuals are attacked by someone who means them harm, the only response they have is their most basic, reactionary instinct, which is usually more harmful than helpful in a self-defense situation.

However, martial arts have kata and drills. A kata is a pre-arranged sequence of motions one memorizes and rehearses like a dance. Drills are single, repetitious moves and motions specifically designed to train the body to do something instinctively. Each time the martial artist practices the kata or a drill, they visualize the attacks these movements defend. They repeat and rehearse it over and over until the motion is no longer a result of a cognitive thought process but an intuitive motion that no longer requires a decision before it is executed. This instinctive motion is referred to as muscle memory.

When a trained martial artist is confronted with a speeding fist flying at his face at twenty miles per hour, he doesn't have to wait for the visual input of seeing a fist pass from his optic nerves to his brain. He doesn't have to wait for the brain to evaluate and analyze what attack is coming or what move is a proper response. He doesn't have to wait for the cognitive process of the brain to send signals to the muscles and limbs telling them to move. A martial artist doesn't need to wait for his muscles to respond to those signals and move into place to meet the attack. Rather, a trained martial artist has rehearsed the response so many times that his muscle memory kicks in. He reacts to meet the threat before his brain has had time to think about it.

Daniel was a man in the Bible who understood this concept. He was thrown into a den of hungry lions to be executed. But let's back up. The lions are the threat. He didn't decide in the den of lions what his reaction would be. In that moment, he didn't go looking for the power of God to intervene in his situation.

The Bible says he'd been praying next to his open window three times a day long before he was thrown into that den. Daniel had been practicing his kata. He had an active, ongoing habit of connecting with God. When his political competitors made it illegal to pray, he prayed anyway. He understood how vital it was to his survival. Even under threat of execution, he knew that giving up his connection to God in prayer was far more dangerous.

I know what some of you are thinking: prayer put him in the lion's den in the first place! Actually, he was targeted by his political competitors because they were jealous of Daniel's favor with the king. If they hadn't targeted his prayer habits, they would have found another opportunity to trap him. They had it out for him whether or not he prayed. If it hadn't been prayer, it would have been something else.

Daniel already had a wide and direct conduit of God's power and favor flowing freely in his life as demonstrated by his consistent success in everything he touched. When he landed on the floor of that pit, he'd practiced his intimate connection to God so often that the lions didn't have a chance. His spiritual muscle memory kicked in, and the power of God was right at his fingertips to save him. Fear didn't control him. Had the pit been the first time he had asked God for help, the fear of the moment might have blocked any connection or access he had to God's power in the situation.

Once again, don't wait until you need help before you decide your response. Prayer allows you to practice connecting with Jesus before you need him, so when you really need him you're already connected. You don't have to go looking for his power.

The Super Bowl is the biggest championship game in American football. They say the Super Bowl isn't won in the game, it's won in the practice. You and I wouldn't stand a chance on the field of the Super Bowl. The athletes who train and beat their bodies into submission on a minute-by-minute basis every day of the season are the ones who win the game. They eat, drink, sleep, breathe, and dream football for eleven months out of the year. You don't decide on game day that you're going to win. It's impossible. Your decision is meaningless because you haven't prepared. You decide to win in your commitment to practice every day.

A student can't decide on test day that they're going to pass the test. They have to study hard in the days and weeks leading up to the test. A driver shouldn't wait until their car is leaking, seizing up, and bursting into flames to take it in for an oil change. Regular maintenance must take place for a car to run properly.

Prayer is not something you do when you need Jesus; prayer is something you practice so that when you need him, you already have him.

SECTION 6: WATER QUALITY MATTERS

There is a wrong way to pray. When in a survival situation, knowing you need water is only a fraction of the battle. Knowing where and how to get it is far more important.

WATER SOURCE

Flowing water is made pure by its movement. Stagnant water doesn't have enough oxygen and movement to filter out or kill harmful substances. In outdoor survival you must seek flowing water sources.

How are you getting your prayer in? Is it intimate and alone or sporadic and detached? Do you seek out flowing sources of conversation, or are you sitting stagnant throughout the week, waiting for Sunday to roll around and give you your Jesus fix for the week?

Consider Jesus's words in Luke 13:25–30:

> "Once the owner of the house gets up and closes the door, you will stand outside knocking and pleading, 'Sir, open the door for us.'
>
> "But he will answer, 'I don't know you or where you come from.'
>
> "Then you will say, 'We ate and drank with you, and you taught in our streets.'
>
> "But he will reply, 'I don't know you or where you come from. Away from me, all you evildoers!'
>
> "There will be weeping there, and gnashing of teeth, when you see Abraham, Isaac and Jacob and all the prophets in the kingdom of God, but you yourselves thrown out. People will come

from east and west and north and south, and will take their places at the feast in the kingdom of God. Indeed there are those who are last who will be first, and first who will be last."

To that Scripture I would add a modern rephrasing: "'I went to church! I sang all the songs! I volunteered in the nursery,' and he will reply, 'I don't know you. That was spending time near me, not spending time with me.'"

Some Jews thought that because of their heritage, religious institutions, and proximity to the things of God, they had intimacy with him. They were in for a terrifying wake-up call, and so are we if we think that once-a-week prayers are impressing God.

PURITY

Water can harbor any number of viruses, bacteria, parasites, and infectious diseases that can kill you without the help of being stranded in the wild.

How pure are your prayers? What are your motives? Why are you praying?

Pride, selfishness, vindictive anger, greed, and arrogance are just a few of the harmful substances that can poison your prayers to not only prevent them from being beneficial, but actually harm your relationship with God. Remember James 4:6: "God opposes the proud but shows favor to the humble."

In Luke 18:9–14, Jesus tells a story that illustrates how God doesn't respond well to prayers prayed from a poisoned attitude:

> To some who were confident of their own righteousness and looked down on everyone else, Jesus told this parable: "Two men went up to the temple to pray, one a Pharisee and the other a tax collector. The Pharisee stood by himself and prayed: 'God, I thank you that I am not like other people—robbers, evildoers, adulterers—or even like this tax collector. I fast twice a week and give a tenth of all I get.'
>
> "But the tax collector stood at a distance. He would not even look up to heaven, but beat his breast and said, 'God, have mercy on me, a sinner.'

"I tell you that this man, rather than the other, went home justified before God. For all those who exalt themselves will be humbled, and those who humble themselves will be exalted."

SALT WATER

If you find seawater, drinking that salt water can dehydrate you much faster. Your body needs salt, but when you consume too much salt, your body's solution is to flush it out using whatever fluids are left in your system. When you drink salt water, you're losing more water than you're taking in.

Are you drinking the right *kind* of water? Are your prayers the right kind of prayers? The wrong kind of prayer produces no results and could damage your faith.

There's no point in praying for things that God cannot give. God cannot make people do things, give you something sinful, or deliver you from the natural consequences of your ongoing choices. If doing drugs is killing you, God is not going to heal you until you choose to stop doing drugs.

You don't need to pray for things God has already given through his promises. There are thousands of if-then statements in the Bible. *If* you do this, *then* I will do that. We could be praying for things that God has already told us how to obtain through nothing more than simple obedience. Deuteronomy 28 is a good example. So is Simon's earnest, errant attempt at trying to buy the Holy Spirit:

> When Simon saw that the Spirit was given at the laying on of the apostles' hands, he offered them money and said, "Give me also this ability so that everyone on whom I lay my hands may receive the Holy Spirit." Peter answered: "May your money perish with you, because you thought you could buy the gift of God with money! You have no part or share in this ministry, because your heart is not right before God" (Acts 8:18–21).

Simon was trying to obtain a free gift from God by paying money instead of through a personal relationship with Jesus. Wrong prayer! You can't circumvent a relationship with Jesus to obtain what you want.

CONTAMINANTS

Even if you sanitize water to kill harmful organisms, there can still be contaminants in the water such as animal waste, chemicals, garbage, and toxic runoff.

Living with unrepentant sin is a sure way to poison the waters of prayer, even if your prayer is genuinely pure. If you are living in sin that you're not even trying to address, or if you're unapologetically doing things you know are wrong, that's like a child asking politely for a piece of candy just after he spat in your face. He may have asked correctly, but it followed actions that demanded discipline, not reward.

James 5:16 says, "Therefore confess your sins to each other and pray for each other so that you may be healed. The prayer of a righteous person is powerful and effective." If you want powerful and effective prayers, clear the contaminants through confessing your sins.

FILTRATION

If you find the right water and filter out the contaminants, you'll have something safe and beneficial to drink. But the wrong filter might not strain out all of the harmful substances. There are good filters and bad filters.

What's informing and determining what you pray? What filters your prayer? Are *you* determining what you should be praying about? Are you setting yourself up as the expert on prayer that filters out what you should pray about?

In Matthew 26:39, we're told, "Going a little farther, he [Jesus] fell with his face to the ground and prayed, 'My Father, if it is possible, may this cup be taken from me. Yet not as I will, but as you will.'" Jesus brought his request, but he let *God* decide what was going to happen next. God guided his prayers. Even Jesus knew that God is far smarter than we are and he has a much bigger plan and purpose than we can see.

A hamster in a cage can scratch, dig, and climb all day long to escape his cage. He can squeak and send all the cute, pleading looks he wants at his owner. But the owner sees the hungry cat waiting below the cage for the hamster to escape. Sometimes I think God hears our prayers and says, "Child, I see a bigger picture here. If I give you what you're asking for, it will destroy you."

Prayers work much better if we filter them through what *God* wants for our lives. He's smarter than we are and sees a much bigger picture than we do.

SECTION 7: THE RIGHT WAY TO PRAY

If you want to play sports like a pro, study the pro's playbook. No one knew how to pray better than Jesus himself. We don't have to ask him how we should pray; Jesus's disciples asked the question for us. I think we should pay attention to the expert's advice. In answering the question of how to pray, Jesus gave us the example that we call the Lord's Prayer. It's found in Matthew 6:5-13 and most of us are familiar with it. Let's fully analyze this passage to see the master strategy that the King of Kings gave to guide our prayers.

1. Get alone with God.
"And when you pray, do not be like the hypocrites, for they love to pray standing in the synagogues and on the street corners to be seen by others. Truly I tell you, they have received their reward in full. But when you pray, go into your room, close the door and pray to your Father, who is unseen. Then your Father, who sees what is done in secret, will reward you." Make sure you find an intentional time you can be alone to give God your exclusive attention.

2. Fancy words don't make prayers better, neither does repetition.
"And when you pray, do not keep on babbling like pagans, for they think they will be heard because of their many words. Do not be like them, for your Father knows what you need before you ask him." No magic words make prayer more effective. Even repeating this very prayer that Jesus prayed doesn't have any inherent properties that make it work better.

3. Praise God.

"Our Father in heaven, hallowed be your name." We'll address worship in more detail in a following chapter, but if praising and worshiping God should be a part of everything you do, how much more should praising God be incorporated into your conversations with God? Just spend time in the conversation thanking him for his blessings, giving him credit for the good he's done, and recognizing his amazing attributes.

4. Ask for what God wants.

"Your kingdom come, your will be done, on earth as it is in heaven." Think about how God's will is done in heaven. Do you think God has to do anything other than express what he wants before it comes to be? God says it, it happens. There's no debate and no reasons are given. What God wants just happens in heaven. God's kingdom is wherever his will is being accomplished in perfect order. Imagine if that's what you had in your life. No one knows better than God the best possible plan in every situation.

5. Pray for your daily needs.

"Give us today our daily bread." God wants you to ask for the things you need. If you have a need, bring it to God. As long as asking for stuff isn't the only thing you do, there's nothing wrong with asking.

But more than that, God wants you to daily depend on him for all of your provisions. When the Israelites escaped Egypt and had to wander in the wilderness, God provided them food in the form of manna, a substance that appeared every morning and went bad by the following day. God told them to gather as much as they needed for the day but no more, or it would spoil. When you recognize that you must depend on his provision day-by-day, you never forget the source of your provision.

6. Pray for forgiveness.

"And forgive us our debts [sins]." We are not perfect. God expects us to fail, not because he wants us to, but because he knows we're in a struggle against our worldly natures. When we fall, we admit it, get back up, and try again. When we fail, he's waiting for us to come to him for healing and not to isolate ourselves or ignore the problem. If we are going to have his help overcoming sin, we have to bring that sin to him to be overcome.

7. Pray against temptation.

"And lead us not into temptation, but deliver us from the evil one." The Devil is far out of our league, and he's relentless. I don't know anyone who has much luck trying to will their way to overcoming their own dark and sinful nature. This evil world and its influence in our lives isn't taking a vacation any time soon. Why fight that battle? We can't possibly survive without God's influence in our day to protect us from these kinds of unending attacks.

8. Pray for others.
Although it wasn't detailed in this particular prayer that Jesus prayed, we find that Jesus and the disciples frequently prayed for others. In John 17, Jesus prays a very long and passionate prayer for his disciples and all future believers who will follow them, including you. Praying for others is called intercession. We stand in the gap and plead to God for the benefit of someone else. Sometimes we need to be like the friends who brought their crippled buddy to Jesus on a mat. When the friends found a crowd blocking them from getting into the house, they carried their buddy up to the roof and dropped him through the ceiling to make sure his need was laid right at the feet of Jesus.

SECTION 8: MY EXPERIENCE

I hope that my example that follows can be an illustration of the kind of things you can do in personalizing your own conversation time with God. My prayer time is personalized to the way I best connect with God, what I need to pray, and how I need to pray it.

This isn't a formula or pattern that I think is worth recommending to someone else. That would be like assuming that the conversations I enjoy with my wife and kids should be the same conversations everyone else should have with their families. Take what you read out of the Word of God and perhaps use this book as a guideline, but personalize your own prayer time to the best way you connect with God. Besides, what I pray about changes as my relationship with God grows. Some things that used to be a daily struggle aren't the same challenges I face today. As new needs arise, my prayers mature.

When I completely committed to making Bible reading and prayer a part of my daily routine, I needed something to keep my mind focused. I needed certain things I prayed every day to make sure I had a complete conversation with God every day. As of the writing of this book, my morning prayer includes:

A. Waking up before my family to pray. (Get alone with God.)
B. Submission and surrender. (Praise God, and ask for what God wants.)
C. Praying on the Armor of God from Ephesians 6. (Pray against temptation.)

D. Prayer for persecuted believers and missionaries. (Pray for others.)
E. Intercession for the needs of others and myself. (Pray for others, and pray for your needs.)
F. Prayer in tongues. (Ask for what God wants.)
G. Prayer over what I'm about to read in the Bible. (Ask for what God wants, and pray for your needs.)
H. I listen to God as I study my Bible. (More on this in the next chapter.)

WHAT'S NEXT?

This chapter has an assignment. Without a decision, an action, and something in place to keep you accountable to that decision, it's highly unlikely that you will alter your current patterns of behavior.

1. Decide now when and where you can pray each day for at least thirty minutes.

Physically write it down so you can feel it with your pen and look at it with your eyes. What time of day and in what place of your home are you going to pray?

2. Find someone to hold you accountable. Preferably, find someone who also wants to make daily prayer a priority in their lives. Any significant change in habit requires accountability. For example, have the other person text you every morning at six to make sure you're awake, or have them call you every afternoon at five when you both get off work, or have them check in on you at church every week. Admit to one another how much you've prayed throughout the week. Get a partner.

3. Make prayer your number one priority. Remember, prayer affects every area of every part of your life, including the other components in this survival kit. Nothing is more important in life than prayer. In order to give it the priority it deserves, you should literally treat prayer as equally important as water in your life, because without water your body dies. But without prayer, your eternal soul could die.

Stay connected to the vine.

CHAPTER 3: WE NEED FOOD

BIBLE STUDY

Before reading this next chapter I think it's only fitting to start with a passage from the Bible. Read it and ponder its meaning. Think about it deeply as you read and don't read any further until you feel you can fully appreciate it.

> *Blessed* are those whose ways are blameless,
>   who *walk* according to the law of the Lord.
> *Blessed* are those who *keep* his statutes
>   and *seek* him with *all* their heart—
> they do no wrong
>   but *follow* his ways.
> You have laid down precepts
>   that are to be *fully* obeyed.
> Oh, that *my* ways were steadfast
>   in *obeying* your decrees!
> Then I would *not* be put to shame
>   when I *consider* all your commands.
> I will *praise* you with an *upright* heart
>   as I *learn* your righteous laws.
> I will *obey* your decrees;
>   do not utterly forsake me (Psalm 119:1–8, emphasis added).

If you want to fully appreciate the power and purpose of God's Word in your life, I encourage you to read Psalm 119 in its entirety. This excerpt barely begins to touch on the profound truths of this chapter.

Let's review:

1. You're already in a survival situation, so you need to continually prepare because you're never ready.
2. Prayer is our water. If we get it, we live. If we don't, we die.
3. If we remain connected to Jesus, "The Vine," in prayer, we get the flow of his living water. Apart from him we can do nothing
4. There is a wrong and right way to pray. Prayer should be an intimate conversation.
5. Have you followed through with the assignment from the previous chapter and found a time and place to pray, an accountability partner, and made prayer your number one priority in life? If not, stop here, do not read on, and follow through with one thing before picking up another.

I'm about to ask you a few more questions. Be honest with yourself and think about what you really do from day to day. There's no reason to feel bad or good about your answers. This is just the starting point. Before you determine where you're going, you have to determine where you are.

1. How often do you read your Bible for yourself? (Outside of sermons, devotional books, etc.)
2. Do you have many Scriptures memorized and ready for immediate use?
3. Are you satisfied with the amount of time you spend in Bible study? Why or why not?

SECTION 1: THE NEED FOR FOOD

If prayer is your water, then the Bible is certainly your food. If you remember, you can only go a matter of a few days without water. You can go about thirty to forty-five days without food before your body starves to death. Like lacking water, this timeframe greatly depends on many factors, such as your beginning health, environmental hazards, liquid intake, etc. It is a basic physiological fact that your body needs food. This is assumed as true by everyone because everyone has felt hunger.

Why don't people assume the same to be true of the Bible? I believe it's because they don't recognize the symptoms of spiritual hunger or the true source of spiritual food that God has provided.

Before proceeding, let's establish something very important. Everything I'm about to cover in this chapter is based on an assumption. Nothing will hit home unless you believe **all of the Bible is true.**

It's the right nutrition—not just some of it, and not just the parts we like, but all of it. If only parts of the Bible were true, who decides which parts are worth believing?

I learned all of the following from Junior Bible Quiz as a child, through Bible College, and through my own private study. Consider it a crash course in why to believe the Bible is true. This is only a taste. Many complete books have more thorough explanations. These are just some of my favorites:

- Third-party sources and eyewitness accounts outside of Scripture confirm many of the reports spoken of in Scripture.
- Archaeological findings have repeatedly confirmed events spoken of in Scripture.
- The Bible's timelessness and endurance through the millennia lends credence to its authenticity.

- The Bible's impact on the hearts and lives of billions of people cannot be ignored.
- Thousands of fulfilled prophesies are in the Bible, showing that what it *says* is going to happen *will* happen. Over three hundred Old Testament prophesies were fulfilled in Jesus's life and death alone!

Even more telling, the Bible was written over a period of about 1,600 years by about forty different authors from varied walks of life, from kings to peasants and doctors to fishermen, most of whom didn't know one another or have access to each other's writings. They all wrote about one topic, God's relationship with man, yet there are no contradictions. They all agree with one another. Statistically, that's impossible unless they were all writing from a single source of information, God himself.

Let me put that one in perspective: imagine collecting forty random people and isolating them in different rooms to write a book on how to train dogs. Each would write their individual opinion on dog training methods. If you collected the results into a single volume, how do you think it would fare among dog training books?

You would have forty different versions of how to train a dog, many of which directly disagreed with each other. Now, add the chronological and cultural barriers the biblical authors had and you get a Bible that must have been authored by God through people. It would have been impossible for the authors to agree—unless God gave them the words.

In summary, the Bible is inspired. God inspired each word of the Bible and not just its thoughts and ideas. It's *all* true. As 2 Timothy 3:16 reminds us, "All Scripture is God-breathed and is useful for teaching, rebuking, correcting and training in righteousness." Some other religious texts may try to boast one of the things on this list as proof of their validity, but only the Bible fulfills them all.

In other words, The Bible is true, it's written by God himself, and therefore has every right and authority to tell us how to live our lives. In fact, more than that, it's the *only* way we should live our lives.

SECTION 2: FOOD SOURCE

Since we're talking about our need for food, I have to tell you about my ungrateful children. Oh, don't get me wrong. I love them dearly, but sometimes they underappreciate the blessings they've been given.

Every Sunday I take my kids to an all-you-can-eat buffet. I let them eat as much of anything they want. I don't say no to anything they ask for. Appetizers, drinks, side dishes, deserts—it's all there for them.

When they tell me they can't eat any more, I pay the bill from my hard-earned money and we go home.

But six hours later, these ungrateful kids have the nerve to ask me for more food. Of course, I tell them that if they wanted more food, they should have taken another plate at the buffet when they had a chance.

When the next day rolls around, the kids are still asking me for more food. They whine and complain and moan about how hungry they are, completely ungrateful for the limitless amount of food I gave them access to the day before. This pattern of whining for food continues all week long until Sunday rolls around again and I take them back to the buffet. Then each week I remind them that this is the only meal they're getting this week, so they had better eat enough to last them until next Sunday or don't bother complaining.

The above story is obviously *not* true. If I treated my children this way, I'd be considered an abuser and rightfully lose custody of them. But isn't that what we do with our spiritual meals?

Don't we say something like this: *Give me a microwavable spiritual meal that I can get into an hour-and-fifteen-minute service on a Sunday Morning. Make forty minutes of it song time so I can worship and feel good, leaving only thirty minutes left for the preaching of the Word, only seven minutes of which is actually speaking the Word itself. Fill the rest of the time with anecdotal illustrations to keep my interest and please explain how I can apply the information because I cannot figure that out for myself anymore.*

I know that's a gross generalization, but have we reduced our spiritual food to this microwave meal in order to feed our entire week? Sunday sermons are awesome, but if they're your only source of spiritual food every week, you're starving and you don't even know it. No wonder self-help books are one of the biggest sections in the bookstores, even Christian bookstores. People would rather listen to TV evangelists, read books, and go to counselors than study to understand the instruction manual for themselves. It's easier to call technical support to fix the problem than to read the instructions for yourself.

I have a friend I used to work with named James. He's one of the brightest and most practically intelligent men I know. One of his duties was to take on all I.T. and technical support for the office and its computers. As anyone with a computer knows, every computer had a problem almost every week.

The thing I appreciated most about James was also the thing I hated the most about him. When you gave him your computer problem, he pointed you to where *you* could find the solution. He didn't get out of his chair to go sit behind your desk and fix the computer. Rather, he sent you a link to a tutorial on how to fix the problem. He gave you the tools to fix it yourself.

This method did three things.

First, it allowed him to focus his attention on more immediate and more serious responsibilities he was obligated to fill instead of wasting time fixing problems other people were fully capable of fixing themselves.

Second, it gave the solution to the person who needed it in a way that if the problem ever came up again, that person already had the solution.

Third, it annoyed me because it meant I had to take responsibility, grow, and learn to do something for myself.

If he was to get any work done, it was not only the best way for him to handle problems, it was the *only* way. To his credit, if we couldn't figure it out for ourselves, he was still willing to come in and do it for us, but he always gave us the opportunity to fix it ourselves first before he came in to evaluate it further.

We hate taking responsibility. It's hard work, so we've taken the lazy route. "Can't someone else do it for me?" We've delegated feeding ourselves to those we believe are our spiritual betters. We sit wearing bibs like forty-year-old babies in our sagging high chairs waiting for mommy and daddy pastors to spoon-feed us Bible mush that's easy to digest. When are we going to pick up the fork and knife and feed ourselves some solid food?

The point is, it's easier to take the American approach to let someone else prepare all your needs for you so you don't have to do the hard work of preparing your own daily meals. God's Word is not something you stockpile for a long winter of no food. God's Word is something you daily harvest because it needs to stay fresh in your life. There are no shortcuts or easy answers.

That's why Jesus says in the Lord's prayer in Matthew 6:11, "Give us this day our *daily* bread." Yesterday's supply has already run dry, and today's supply will not last through tomorrow. Today, give me today's portions to make it through *this* day. And I'll come to you again tomorrow for tomorrow's portion.

This practice of a daily harvest began in Exodus 16:3–31:

> The Israelites said to them, "If only we had died by the Lord's hand in Egypt! There we sat around pots of meat and ate all the food we wanted, but you have brought us out into this desert to starve this entire assembly to death."
>
> Then the Lord said to Moses, "I will rain down bread from heaven for you. The people are to go out each day and gather enough for that day. In this way I will

test them and see whether they will follow my instructions. On the sixth day they are to prepare what they bring in, and that is to be twice as much as they gather on the other days. . . ."

That evening quail came and covered the camp, and in the morning there was a layer of dew around the camp. When the dew was gone, thin flakes like frost on the ground appeared on the desert floor. When the Israelites saw it, they said to each other, "What is it?" For they did not know what it was. . . .

Then Moses said to them, "No one is to keep any of it until morning."

However, some of them paid no attention to Moses; they kept part of it until morning, but it was full of maggots and began to smell. So Moses was angry with them. . . .

The people of Israel called the bread manna. It was white like coriander seed and tasted like wafers made with honey.

God's plan for the Israelites was that they needed to come to him every day for their daily provision. This was and still is our daily reminder of our dependence on him and none other.

If you're not getting your dose daily, you're starving your soul.

SECTION 3: LIGHT MY PATH

"Your word is a lamp for my feet, a light on my path" (Psalm 119:105).

Many people pack a survival kit with navigational supplies: a compass, GPS, map, etc. I confess that I'm hopeless with directions. God never connected those wires in my head. Some people are directionally challenged. I'm directionally inept. I get lost on the way to my own closet. I *need* to pack navigational supplies.

But there are still responsibilities in using these items. Manufacturers try to make it easy, but some GPS systems (especially off-road types) are complicated and electronic, which means technical difficulties can arise, such as power loss or damage. Compasses and maps are helpful, but only if you know how to use them. I confess: I've taught the compass merit in my boy's Royal Ranger club. I spent four weeks teaching the material straight out of the book and I still struggle with how to use a compass properly.

Navigational equipment is smart. But wouldn't it be useful and even prudent to pack an instructional guidebook on how to use all of the navigational equipment?

Let's say I put all of these navigational objects in my survival pack and blindly headed out with my buddy into the wilderness without using any of the tools in my pack. I'd get us completely lost!

First of all, if I consulted the objects in my pack, I might not get lost in the first place. I might be able to recognize the proper destination and the proper route to get there. Second, let's say I begin stumbling among hazards in my journey, putting us at increasingly more risk. Let's say I go as far as to get us into life-threatening peril by choosing the wrong direction. Should I ask my buddy what he thinks we should do? No. He's just as lost and confused as I am. Should I try to think and reason my way out of peril? No. That's what got me into peril in the first place. Should I pray and ask God to miraculously deliver me from my own stupidity? No! I'm suffering the consequences of my own decisions.

God has already given me the tools to get me out. He's not going to help me until I use what he's already provided!

This reminds me of an old joke. A heavy rainstorm is threatening to flood a neighborhood. A neighbor drives up to a homeowner in the rising waters and offers to give him a ride out of town. The homeowner refuses and says, "I'm a Christian. I've prayed. God will save me."

The waters flood the streets. A boat floats by and those inside offer him a ride. Again, the homeowner refuses and says, "I'm a Christian. I've prayed. God will save me."

The floods rise. He climbs to his roof and prays for God to deliver him. A rescue helicopter flies by and throws him a rope. He refuses and says, "I'm a Christian. I've prayed. God will send me a miracle."

The waters rise, sweep him away, and he dies.

He gets to heaven and says to God, "I prayed and put all my faith in you. Why didn't you come and save me?"

God says, "I sent you a car, boat, and a helicopter. What more were you looking for?"

In other words, if you're not opening the Bible, reading it, and using it, it's not actually doing you any good.

Growing up, my karate teacher, Dave Pearson, was a profound influence on my life. Dave is a godly man and collected lots of short, memorable truths that still stick with me:

"A dusty Bible leads to a dirty life."

"You can tell a person's life is not falling apart if their Bible is."

"The Word of God is the only weapon that gets sharper with use."

SECTION 4: THE SWORD

The Word of God is also your sword of the Spirit. The Bible is referred to as a sword, and the only offensive weapon, in the armor of God described in Ephesians 6. Imagine going into battle with nothing but defensive armor. How foolish would a soldier have to be to walk into a war zone with a bulletproof vest, equipment belt, helmet, and combat boots, but leave his gun in the tent?

Remember, you're under constant, relentless attack by the enemy of your soul. You must defend yourself and you must also fight back. The Word of God is the provided, standard-issue weapon of choice.

"For the word of God is alive and active. Sharper than any double-edged sword, it penetrates even to dividing soul and spirit, joints and marrow; it judges the thoughts and attitudes of the heart" (Hebrews 4:12). The Word of God is alive and sharper than a sword. A physical sword can only cut my flesh, but the Word of God is so sharp it can cut straight to my soul.

"The weapons we fight with are not the weapons of the world. On the contrary, they have divine power to demolish strongholds. We demolish arguments and every pretension that sets itself up against the knowledge of God, and we take captive every thought to make it obedient to Christ" (2 Corinthians 10:4–5).

A sword is only good if you pull it *out* of its sheath. If it stays closed it does me no good and I'll die in battle. A Bible does you no good sitting unused on your shelf. You have to *read* it.

A sword is only good if you *know* how to use it. Pulling out my sword does me no good if I've never learned how it works. I can hold the right weapon and still die in battle. Reading the Bible isn't enough. You have to *study* it to know what it means.

A sword is only good if it's *sharp*. Even if I knew the moves, I would waste a lot of energy swinging a dull sword because it would never stop the enemy. All he would have to do is wait me out. Eventually I would tire, get overpowered, and die. Studying the Bible isn't enough. You have to *understand* how it applies to your life.

A sword is only good if you *actually* use it. I can have all the head knowledge, skills, practice, and tools to fight, but if I don't actually raise my arm and swing the thing in a fight, I'm going to die. Understanding the Bible isn't enough. You have to *apply* and *obey* it for it to do any good.

A sword is only good if you have it *with* you. Even a master swordsman who's practiced with the finest sword and has the will to swing it will die if the sword is left in its display case at home. Applying the Bible isn't enough. When you're under pressure, you need to have it *memorized* so you can access the truth when you really need it.

In Matthew 4 and Luke 4, we see Jesus attacked with temptation in the wilderness. Each time he was tempted, Jesus fought back with Scripture. When the enemy told him to turn the stones into bread to feed his flesh, Jesus focused not on his fleshly desires but on his spiritual survival needs. He quoted Deuteronomy 8:3, "No! The Scriptures say, 'People do not live by bread alone, but by every word that comes from the mouth of God.'" He saw that his spiritual survival and need for the bread of God's words was far more important than the food the body needs. He knew that the Scripture he memorized was on hand and ready to use in battle. He knew and lived Psalm 119:11: "I have hidden your word in my heart that I might not sin against you."

In other words, memorize Scripture.

As a Jewish rabbi, Jesus had the entire Old Testament memorized. If he followed the pattern of his culture, and we have every indication that he did, he had the first five books of the Bible memorized by age twelve—not the names of the books, but their actual contents! And before you object, it was *not* because he wrote the book. In coming to earth he emptied himself of his divinity. Though he was fully God, he was God in human form and had to learn everything he knew the same way we do. Luke 2:52 says, "Jesus grew in wisdom and in stature," and in John 15:15, Jesus says, "I have called you friends, for everything that I *learned* from my father I have made known to you" (emphasis added).

He actually, factually memorized the Old Testament—for real. And kids are still doing this today in Jewish Yeshiva schools in Jerusalem, New York, and all over the world. Thousands of students still memorize *and* study to understand the Torah and Tanakh, our Old Testament, in two languages.

Don't tell me you can't memorize. It's just not true. Performers such as actors, musicians, and public speakers repeatedly memorize long and complicated presentations. They find a way because it's what they wish to do. Memorize. It's not as impossible as the lies of your flesh have led you to believe.

It's not just for kids either. Don't buy in to the lie that it's easier for a child to memorize than an adult. Adults can memorize too. I was an adult when I memorized Galatians 2:20, Psalm 86:11–13, and Romans 6.

In other words, if you don't have your sword with you when you need to fight, it does you little good.

SECTION 5: HOW TO READ YOUR BIBLE

Similar to prayer, the Bible needs to be integrated into every part of your life. But like prayer, there needs to also be times when it is your only focus and you spend intimate time with God, meditating on the Bible. When I say meditate, I do not mean "meditate" the way some eastern religions do. I like the way Rick Warren described meditation in *The Daniel Plan:*

> In many ways, biblical meditation is the exact opposite of eastern or New Age meditation, which is about emptying your mind and repeating a single word or mantra. In contrast, biblical meditation means taking a verse of the Bible, such as a promise or a command or a story, and seriously pondering its meaning.

Like we established earlier, it does you no good to simply read words on a page. You have to study, understand, and apply it as well. You need an intimate relationship with God and his Word if you are to actually have a functional tool in your survival kit.

Here are some guidelines for your intimate time meditating on God's Word:

1. Pick a quiet place and time. (Just like your prayer time.)
2. Make a plan. For example, read through the Gospels, read a chronological Bible, or follow a pre-determined reading plan. The point is that you see Scripture in whole portions with complete context and not just in random segments.
3. Pray before you read. Ask God to speak to you and help you understand.
4. Read the Bible.
5. Mark or highlight verses that speak to you. It's okay to write in your Bible.
6. Keep a notebook and write down verses or thoughts that seem significant to you.
7. Pray more. Thank God for speaking to you.

The day you stop searching for a deeper understanding and pursuit of Christ is the day you start dying. Life with God is a treadmill. He never stops moving forward. If you stop moving forward, you'll fall off the back.

SECTION 6: MY EXPERIENCE

My experience in this area is simple. I memorized a lot of Scripture as a child and I use that memorized Scripture daily. I use it internally as I pray and as I live out my choices. I use it externally in my conversations with others. The Bible is my answer to every troubling question and my response to every temptation.

As I became an adult, I realized that I could still memorize Scripture. As a child I memorized what I was assigned, but the Scripture I memorized as an adult was more personal. They were Scriptures that meant something significant to me in my life. I also realized that the more I read the Bible, the more I loved it. As I read more consistently, so many truths started jumping out at me from the pages. I would laugh and I would cry as I read. I fell in love.

I've heard similar experiences from others. The more we read the Bible, the more it comes alive. It speaks to us. It gets inside of us and changes who we are for the better. Believe me when I say that if you find Bible reading boring, you're either doing it wrong or not doing it enough, because it has become one of the foundational pillars of joy and satisfaction both in my relationship with God and in my life in general.

WHAT'S NEXT?

This chapter also has an assignment. Without a decision, an action, and something in place to keep you accountable to that decision, it is highly unlikely that you will alter your current pattern of behavior. Don't forget to include your accountability partner in all of your lifestyle decisions.

1. Continue your intimate thirty-plus minutes of prayer each day. Do not pick up the Bible at the expense of prayer. You need both. Continue praying at the time and place you determined in the last chapter.

2. Choose a quiet place and time for where and when you will study the Bible each day. Most people's intimate time studying the Word of God is in the same time and place as their intimate prayer time, but different people have different lifestyles and sometimes they're not the same. The point is that you need a quiet place to study the Bible just like you need a quiet place to pray.

3. Study and memorize the Bible for more than thirty minutes each day. Remember, studying the Bible is your spiritual food. Don't starve your soul throughout the week waiting for Sunday's buffet. Feeding your spirit is worth giving up something less crucial so you have time to do it right. If you have to sacrifice something in life, don't let it be the essentials to survival such as Bible reading and prayer.

CHAPTER 4: WE NEED FIRE

WORSHIP

Before you read this next chapter, I'd like to stop and remind you of something vital. The survival kit for your soul, your essentials for life, is a relationship with Jesus. Relationships are not built on rules. They are built on love. God loves you. God wants your love in return. Reading your Bible and praying should be birthed out of a desire to know your Heavenly Father and discern his perfect desires for your life. None of this should ever become about checking off the hour of devotional prayer and Bible from your daily to-do list.

The relationship also won't dissolve if you forget to read your Bible for a day, or if you occasionally have an intimate time far shorter than usual. This book is not about salvation issues; it's about survival issues. You can go three days without water and a month without food. You don't immediately die when you skip dinner once in a while. So please do not get discouraged or give up if you cannot keep up the pace of an hour of Bible reading and prayer. When you forget a day or are forced to shorten your normal routine, just hop back on the next day, or whenever you and your accountability partner can get back on track. As you read this chapter, you'll discover that without an attitude of worshipful devotion to God, mechanical habits can lead you into nothing more than empty, impersonal religion. Everything is supposed to grow out of your love and devotion to your Heavenly Father.

Let's review:

1. You're already in a survival situation, so you need to continually prepare because you're never ready.
2. If you remain connected to Jesus, "The Vine," in prayer, you get the flow of his living water. Apart from him, you can do nothing.
3. A once-a-week buffet is not enough to sustain you. You have to feed your spirit daily with the Word of God.
4. Studying the instructions and training with your sword equips you for battle. Unused tools are useless.
5. A sword is only good if it's with you. Memorize Scripture.

So, in light of this review, have you been consistently reading your Bible and praying? If so, has it had a dramatic impact on your actions and outlook on life? Remember how your intimate time with God affects your life. Remembering will help you stick with it for the rest of your life. If you have not been consistent, why are you reading this book? Your spiritual and eternal survival is far too vital for excuses. Just do it. Start now.

I'm about to ask you the opening evaluation questions. Be honest with yourself and think about what you really do from day to day. There's no reason to feel bad or good about your answers. This is just the starting point. Before you determine where you're going, you have to determine where you are.

1. Why do you serve Jesus?
2. How do you worship?
3. Can you think of any part of Christian life that is *not* worship?

SECTION 1: HOW MUCH IS GOD WORTH?

How much do you think my wedding ring is worth? In order to find out, you might ask questions about what the ring is made out of, how big it is, and where I bought it. I could find the receipt and tell you how much money was spent to purchase it, but it was also a gift from someone I love. My wedding ring is a symbol of my marriage to my wife. She gave it to me on our wedding day. That makes it worth more to me than just the money I spent on it. It has sentimental value. I have an emotional attachment to it. So, this ring is worth the money I spent on it plus my sentimental attachment to what it means to me.

How much is your television worth? A couple of hundred dollars perhaps? Well, it's certainly worth more than that. You may spend hours upon hours in front of it. Most people spend more time watching TV than they do eating. That means the TV is worth not only money, but also time. By watching TV for hours on end, people show that it is worth investing their time into it.

How much is a football worth? Many people play sports. What would you say your sports or hobbies are worth? Well, you obviously spend time on them. You also invest your energy. TV takes your time, but sports are worth more than just time. They're worth time, effort, practice, energy, and sometimes even injury. If athletes get hurt, do they quit and never play again? No. They keep working to recovery and get back into the game; they show that their sport is worth injury.

What is God worth? Is he worth your time? Is he worth your money? Is he worth your energy? What if you're mocked or even hurt because of your love for Jesus? Is he worth injury? God created the universe. He created you. He gave you life, a home, a family, food, clothing, and if you've asked him to lead your life, he's even forgiven you of your sins and given you eternal life! When it's time to give your tithes and offerings, do you give joyfully, or would you rather spend the money on jewelry? When it's time to pray and read your Bible, do you do it joyfully, or would you rather spend that time in front of the TV? When it's time to sing, dance, clap, and shout in worship, do you do it joyfully, or would you rather spend your time and energy on sports?

God is worth so much more than a ring, TV, and sports.

Jesus told a parable that expressed how much God's kingdom is worth in Matthew 13:44: "The kingdom of heaven is like a treasure hidden in a field. When a man found it, he hid it again, and then in his joy went and sold all he had and bought that field."

So, you see, God is worth everything we have. No part of your life is more valuable than him. That is why worship needs to precede everything you do, to make sure that he remains what's most important in your life.

SECTION 2: WE NEED FIRE

Warmth is a major factor when surviving in the wild. Without warmth it is easy, even in the middle of a desert, to freeze to death in the nighttime chill. But one can never confuse warmth with fire. Warmth is only one thing that fire provides. I can have a space heater, hand warmers, and a hot water bottle with me out in the woods, but they will not cook my food, boil contaminated water, ward off predators, signal rescuers, provide light, or give me the psychological comfort of sitting beside those flickering flames.

Some people are equally confused about worship. Worship is the fire that fuels everything we do; however, it is too often confused with warmth. Singing songs on a Sunday morning in church or on a weekend church retreat can and should give us a wonderfully warm feeling as we emotionally connect with our Creator in unified, corporate worship with other believers. We may even be able to mimic that feeling as we sing along to a meaningful worship song on the radio at home. But the feelings that worship can provide are only one of its functions. Worship can and should make us feel good, as a fire does, but that is *not* why we worship.

We worship because God deserves it. He's earned the right to be worshiped. As your creator, he already deserves every part of your life. But as your Savior and Redeemer, you owe him more than you could ever repay. Your life and everything in it belongs to him.

Even if you received nothing in return, worship should be a part of your nature and your daily, hourly, and minute-by-minute existence. But God also loves you and wants to participate in that worship. That's why you'll receive these wonderful side effects:

1. Expressive worship such as singing, dancing, and meditating on God's Word does feel good and emotionally connects you to your creator.
2. Worship, or the desire to honor God, is what motivates your Bible reading, prayer, and other spiritual pursuits. If it's not motivated by worship, you may become tempted to treat your spiritual disciplines as a mechanical obligation, or give up on them altogether.
3. Worship keeps everything properly submitted to God and in proper balance. If you're doing it for Jesus, you are far less likely to allow pride, selfishness, or other misleading tendencies to inappropriately elevate the wrong attitudes or pursuits in your life.
4. Worship positively affects and improves everything you do. If anything is completely submitted to God in worship, God governs that thing, and he doesn't make mistakes. He always succeeds.
5. Without worship, nothing is done for the right reasons. Think about it. I know of someone who has memorized the entire Bible, is frequently in the church, believes fully in the existence and power of God, believes in Jesus's death and

resurrection, and understands God's influence in our lives better than I do. His name is Satan. It's not just about what you do; it's about why you do it.

SECTION 3: THE POWER OF WORSHIP

Worship is a weapon of warfare. When God is placed first, at the head, at the very forefront of everything you do, his power goes before you and paves the way for his perfect will to be accomplished. No one beats God.

Below are two examples of times when the priests, worship instruments, praises, and shouts of victory were placed at the head of the army. They are living examples of how there is physical power in worship. There is a tangible, observable, victorious effect when God is worshiped first. We conquer physical challenges in the spiritual realm first when God is worshiped.

> So Joshua son of Nun called the priests and said to them, *"Take up the ark of the covenant of the Lord and have seven priests carry trumpets in front of it."* And he ordered the army, "Advance! March around the city, with an armed guard going ahead of the ark of the Lord."

When Joshua had spoken to the people, the seven priests carrying the *seven trumpets before the Lord went forward, blowing their trumpets,* and the ark of the Lord's covenant followed them. . . .

On the seventh day, they got up at daybreak and marched around the city seven times in the same manner, except that on that day they circled the city seven times. The seventh time around, *when the priests sounded the trumpet blast,* Joshua commanded the army, *"Shout!* For the Lord has given you the city! . . .

When the *trumpets sounded, the army shouted,* and at the *sound of the trumpet,* when the men gave a *loud shout,* the wall collapsed; so everyone charged straight in, and they took the city (Joshua 6:6–8, 15–16, 20, emphasis added).

Jehoshaphat *bowed down* with his face to the ground, and all the people of Judah and Jerusalem *fell down in worship* before the Lord. Then some *Levites* from the Kohathites and Korahites stood up and *praised the Lord,* the God of Israel, with a *very loud voice.*

Early in the morning they left for the Desert of Tekoa. As they set out, Jehoshaphat stood and said, "Listen to me, Judah and people of Jerusalem! *Have faith in the Lord* your God and you will be upheld; *have faith* in his prophets and you will be successful." After consulting the people, Jehoshaphat *appointed men to sing to the Lord and to praise him for the splendor of his holiness* as they went out at the head of the army, saying:

> *"Give thanks to the Lord,
> for his love endures forever."*

As they began to *sing and praise,* the Lord set ambushes against the men of Ammon and Moab and Mount Seir who were invading Judah, and they were defeated. The Ammonites and Moabites rose up against the men from Mount Seir to destroy and annihilate them. After they finished slaughtering the men from Seir, they helped to destroy one another (2 Chronicles 20:18–23, emphasis added).

Joshua, as he was commanded by God, placed the Ark of God's presence, the priests, and the trumpets at the front lines of the march around Jericho, they led the whole nation in a shout, and the walls came down for them to overtake their Promised Land. Jehoshaphat worshipped God before going out, placed the worshipers on the front lines, and made sure the entire nation praised God behind them as God fought the entire battle for them. They didn't have to lift a finger and the enemy killed themselves.

When very real terrors plague your life, when battles rage in your home, your workplace, and even your church, you must place the honor of God at the head of the charge. Worship. Praise. Give thanks. Surrender to God. Obey God. When these things come first, the victory can be won before you even approach the battle lines.

Imagine if worship preceded every workday. Imagine if God fought your battles in the spiritual plane before you ever approached it on the physical plane. The Israelites faced real men in armor with swords and arrows who intended to kill them. If God can beat real soldiers when Israel worshiped, God can defeat our little enemies when we worship.

SECTION 4: MISCONCEPTIONS

Unfortunately, our own experiences and other outside influences on our lives mean that there are as many definitions of worship as there are churches in North America. Some people speak and think of only one type of worship so often that we are misled into believing that there is nothing more. Let me help you navigate some of the biggest stumbling points that most people eventually realize.

First, *worship is not just music or singing.* Worship is the motivation that drives our actions. It's who we are, not just something we do. Everything we do can be an expression of worship. "So whether you eat or drink of whatever you do, do it all for the glory of God" (1 Corinthians 10:31).

Singing, especially in a group setting, is merely the *easiest* way to worship. For many, this is a good starting point. But you can sing songs and still live an atrocious life that in no way honors God. If the worship ends when the song does, you're not worshiping, you're playing karaoke.

Second, *church services are not our source of worship.* Church is where we collectively express the worship we have been giving God all week. When church is our primary source of worship, we get very picky about how it's being carried out.

My worship is not dependent on the type of music being played. When I sing in church, it's an expression of what's already happening at home. Arguments about music style, volume, and song selection happen because people depend on that Sunday experience as their main source of worship. If that's your only worship, of course you'll have a strong opinion. Listen: worship God however *you* best connect with him each day at home. Then you'll come to church full, not empty, and be less likely to have problems with the music director's choices.

Take the Israelites as an example of what not to do:

> For I do not want you to be ignorant of the fact, brothers and sisters, that our ancestors were all under the cloud and that they all passed through the sea. They were all baptized into Moses in the cloud and in the sea. They all ate the same spiritual food and drank the same spiritual drink; for they drank from the spiritual rock that accompanied them, and that rock was Christ. Nevertheless, God was not pleased with most of them; their bodies were scattered in the wilderness.

> Now these things occurred as examples to keep us from setting our hearts on evil things as they did (1 Corinthians 10:1–6).

The Israelites experienced the miracles of God as a group, but that didn't mean God was pleased with them. It wasn't personal for most them, and later all they could do was complain. That's why that generation died in the wilderness and never saw the Promised Land

Third, *there is a wrong way to worship.* If done with selfish motives or inconsiderate of the people around you, you are breaking Jesus's two most important commandments to love God and love others. Worship becomes a way to glorify yourself instead of God. If you're just speaking or singing worshipful words to God out of obligation or routine, or to gain something you desire from God, you're not worshipping. "God is spirit, and his worshipers must worship in the Spirit and in truth" (John 4:24).

I have also known people to scream at the top of their lungs in worship, sound a ram's horn trumpet in worship, dance like crazy in worship, and wave any number of flags, tambourines, and hankies in the air. There's nothing inherently wrong with these expressions. In fact, many are spoken of in the Bible. If the whole room was dancing and shouting, it may have been a wonderful and powerful experience, but these individuals were the only ones in the room doing it, and it ripped all the attention off of God and placed it squarely on what they were doing. Regardless of their motives, they were forcing everyone in the room to watch them instead of expressing praise to God.

Recall Paul's admonitions to the Corinthians: "'I have the right to do anything,' you say—but not everything is beneficial. 'I have the right to do anything'—but not everything is constructive. No one should seek their own good, but the good of others" (1 Corinthians 10:23–24). Likewise, "Be careful, however, that the exercise of your rights does not become a stumbling block to the weak" (1 Corinthians 8:9).

Fourth, *mountaintop experiences are not what we seek.* Most Christians at some point in their lives experience what I call a mountaintop experience, a deep, meaningful, and emotional connection with God. It can happen at a camp, a church service, or time spent alone with God. These times can be powerful and life-changing. But think about the heroes of the Bible. Some of them went decades, even lifetimes, between their dynamic experiences with God. We sometimes need those experiences, but we don't live for those experiences.

Remember Dean the evangelist? The area in which he was preaching had just ended a period of drought with a week of hard, heavy rain. The population didn't see the sun for two weeks. It was a bit gloomy. Then the sun finally came out again, and he was viewing the agricultural report on television. The reporter asked a local farmer, "What weather do we need?"

The farmer replied, "We need more rain."

Dean thought this was a bit ungrateful after a week of solid downpour and said as much in his next sermon, only to be corrected by a farmer after the service.

"A torrential gully washer, especially after a long drought, does more damage than good, washing away the topsoil and nutrients the crops need to grow."

Dean was perplexed. "Well, what kind of rain do the crops need?"

"A gentle soaking rain on a regular basis."

We're the same way. Gully washers and emotional mountaintop experiences such as those experienced at church services, camps, and retreats are great, but they can never replace the gentle soaking rain of daily, habitual spiritual disciplines that allow your minute-by-minute life to remain in proper balance with Jesus.

SECTION 5: PROPER WORSHIP

John 4:23–24 reveals what proper worship is: "Yet a time is coming and has now come when the true worshipers will worship the Father in the Spirit and in truth, for they are the kind of worshipers the Father seeks. God is spirit, and his worshipers must worship in the Spirit and in truth."

It's not just about *how* you're worshiping and *what* you're doing, it's a spiritual *motivation* of the heart that produces both *honest and spiritual* worship. Romans 12:1–2 speaks to that motivation: "Therefore, I urge you, brothers and sisters, in view of God's mercy, to offer your bodies as a living sacrifice, holy and pleasing to God—this is your true and proper worship. Do not conform to the pattern of this world, but be transformed by the renewing of your mind. Then you will be able to test and approve what God's will is—his good, pleasing and perfect will."

Worship is sacrificial. It demands that we give up our lives and surrender them to God. We literally die spiritually with Jesus and he lives through us now (Galatians 2:20). We do this through the renewing of our minds into a new way of thinking. True worshipers know that it's not about us anymore. *Everything* is about Jesus, and anything worth anything costs something. *Sacrifice* is a requirement, as 1 Samuel 15:22 shows: "But Samuel replied: 'Does the Lord delight in burnt offerings and sacrifices as much as in obeying the Lord? To obey is better than sacrifice, and to heed is better than the fat of rams.'"

Obedience is the highest form of worship. Worship must include sacrifice such as offerings, time, and talent, but without obedience, sacrifice is meaningless. In other words, you can give to God and still fail because you're not living in obedience. Consider Hebrews 12:2: "Fixing our eyes on Jesus, the pioneer and perfecter of faith. For the joy set before him he endured the cross, scorning its shame, and sat down at the right hand of the throne of God." And also 2 Corinthians 4:18: "So we fix our eyes not on what is seen, but on what is unseen, since what is seen is temporary, but what is unseen is eternal."

This is how you change your perspective. Ignore your senses and the fleeting life in this world and lock your attention on Jesus. *Jesus is the center.*

True and proper worship is always honest, spiritual, sacrificial, obedient, and centered on Jesus. Without these components, it's not worship.

SECTION 6: LIFE VS. ETERNITY

How long do you think you will live? Can you guess how old the oldest person in the Guinness Book of World Records was? One hundred and twenty-two years old. Do you know how old the oldest person in recorded history was? Methuselah, as recorded in the book of Genesis, lived to be 969 years old. The average lifespan in the United States is about seventy-eight years old at the time I'm writing this. Let's say that you beat the average and live to be one hundred years old. That's pretty old isn't it?

Now, picture that you're holding the end of a million-mile-long string. The first three inches of this million-mile string rest in your hands. These first three inches represent your hundred years of life on this earth. These three inches show the time your body will be living on this planet. Not bad. A hundred years seems like a long time. But that's only the first three inches of this very long piece of string.

How long does your spirit last? Forever. Well, how long is forever? It never stops. Eternity keeps going and going for infinity without end. If the rest of the string were your spiritual life in eternity, it could stretch across the room, out the door, and wrap around the earth a billion times and it wouldn't even begin to touch the first blink of eternity.

Now, does this one hundred years on earth look very long? No.

"Why, you do not even know what will happen tomorrow. What is your life? You are a mist that appears for a little while and then vanishes" (James 4:14).

Our life vanishes so fast it seems like a mist, a vapor, a puff of smoke, compared to eternity.

But our entire lives we spend almost all our efforts working to feed our bodies that will only last a hundred years. In just those first three inches of the string, we get an education to get a good job so we can earn money to buy food and shelter and provide for our families. Then we put money aside for our retirement so we can relax when we get old and enjoy the last days of this short life.

We buy stuff to entertain our minds. We eat stuff to stay alive. But our hundred years is all we have to decide what our eternity will look like. What about the rest of your infinitely long string? What are you feeding your spirit? What are you doing in this short life to make sure your spirit will be healthy when it reaches eternity? Once this life is over, your forever is set in stone. You can't go back. You can't change the way your eternity looks once it starts.

With that in mind, which is more important: to feed your body or to feed your spirit? I think it's more important to feed your spirit because your body may only last a hundred years and it's done, a vapor in the wind. But your spirit will last *forever.* So make sure that during the short time you're here on earth you're getting your spiritual food: read your Bible, pray, spend time with God, and live to honor Him. Who cares if it's hard? You'll have the rest of eternity to enjoy life in heaven if your short life is spent feeding your spirit well.

Why include this illustration in a chapter on worship? Worship is all about where your focus lies. Are you doing something for your immediate gratification or for the eternal glory of God?

Worship is about focus. Is your focus on this temporary life on earth or on the spiritual world that controls it? Worship is focus. If your eyes are fixed on the glory and power of almighty God, *everything* melts away as trivial in comparison and *everything* then becomes submitted to that power. As a result, *everything* falls into proper balance and just works better. When life competes with eternity, the focus of worship should be on eternity so God can give you an abundant life now and forevermore.

SECTION 7: PRACTICAL WORSHIP

All of the above sections lay a good philosophical and theological groundwork, but practically speaking, what exactly is one supposed to *do* to worship God? To pray, we lay aside time each day to be intimate and then include Jesus in the eighteen-hour conversation that is the rest of our day. To feed our souls, we set aside time daily to study and memorize the Word so it can be part of every challenge we face. When it comes to worship, here are some things you can do in order to keep your focus in the right place:

- Give something up. Worship is giving. Give your time, money, effort, and sacrifice. Don't give to God that which costs you nothing. That's like giving your mother a free sample as a birthday gift. It's just tacky, and it's not an expression of love.
- Keep your eyes (and life) fixed on the eternal. Include Bible reading and prayer into each day as your "daily bread" reminder that Jesus is really what's most important in life.
- Keep your Bible reading and prayer times productive and in proper balance. It has to be done with the proper attitude of love, worship, and submission to God or it becomes a meaningless routine or a religious exercise devoid of relationship.
- Obey everything the Lord speaks to you out of your time spent with him. Obedience is the highest form of worship.
- Every aspect of your life must become an expression of your love for Jesus. When you work, work that computer program as if God himself gave you the assignment. Your relationships with your boss, your spouse, and your rivals are all with human beings Jesus loved enough to die for. Treat them that way. When you play, let it be an expression of gratitude and love for the

Creator who gave you the freedom to enjoy life. Everything can be done in worship.

SECTION 8: MY EXPERIENCE

Why do I pray? Why do I read my Bible? Why do I go to church? Why do I do anything? It is supposed to be an expression of my love and devotion to God. At the same time, I could pray out of habit, read the Bible out of obligation, and go to church out of peer pressure. For me, the key that determines which version I live is a simple but often very difficult choice.

For years I used to pray, "God help me to . . . ." Fill in the blank with whatever you want. Help me to stop sinning. Help me to do better at school or work. Help me to witness more. I found that I never seemed to get that help. God's answer to that prayer felt like a resounding no. He never seemed to give me the willpower to overcome whatever habit I was trying to change.

Let me explain what I mean. One day, as I was praying a "God, help me to . . . ." prayer, I felt that God said something like this: *Philip, I don't control people. I gave you a free will to choose what you want to do. If I did it for you, I would be stealing your right to choose. I'm never going to make you do anything. You have to choose for yourself what you want to do and just do it. I will give you the power and the ability, but you're the one that has to provide the action. I won't do that for you, so quit asking. This part is your responsibility if you want to change.*

It was then that I realized that some things are purely an act of my own free choice. God is not going to manipulate me like a puppet. I have to move myself. If I want to pray, I am going to have to suck it up and get out of bed when my alarm rings. If I want to quit a bad habit, it's no one's responsibility but my own to decide that I don't want it as a part of my life anymore. That's not to say we cannot obtain help to achieve these things, but ultimately we are responsible for our choices, not God.

Worship, like love, is a choice. Jesus said, "If you love me, obey what I command" (John 14:15). Do I need help to love my wife? Why do I clean the kitchen? Why do I hug her when I come home? Why do I pick up the kids from school? I have chosen to love her. I have chosen to serve her. I can serve my wife out of habit or obligation or peer pressure, but if I want a healthy relationship with my wife, it's my choice and my responsibility to serve her.

When I would lead worship in kids church, I had a live worship band. We would lead songs and try to direct the children into the presence of God. Like any worship leader, there were days when it didn't seem like my young congregation was really connecting with God. There were days I would try to lead them to sing and they would stare at me with blank expressions or wander out of their seats to talk with a friend instead. This occasional experience started to make me think differently when I would worship. When I found myself following my worship leader in the adult service, there would be times I was just mouthing the words without really thinking about what I was singing. I wasn't worshipping either.

Singing is not the only form of worship, but it is by far the easiest. Let's say that someone refuses to worship God at church, with a leader, surrounded by like-minded Christians worshiping to the same song. There is little chance they are worshiping God at home among daily distractions and temptations. If I cannot worship in church during worship time, I doubt I will be worshipful when I am immersed in the world outside of the church.

So I had to make a conscious choice. I chose to do something physical with my body. I chose to take action in order to draw my mind and heart away from other distractions and focus on God. I chose to lift my hands or close my eyes or dance when it was appropriate. Then I found that my choice to act drew my heart into the worship and I was able to connect with God easier.

Then I applied that principle in other areas. When I would pray, I would start by closing my eyes and intentionally focusing on God before I started mindlessly repeating my routine prayer. When I would read my Bible, I would start by physically placing my hand on the pages and asking God to give me insight and understanding into his Word as I read. I chose to let it get inside me and change who I was. This principle of simply stopping to focus on why I was doing things made everything that followed a sincere expression of worship and therefore exponentially more productive.

An easy way to summarize this chapter is to ask, why are you doing what you do? Is it out of obligation or selfish gain, or is it out of a desire to honor God? If you can't proudly lift your voice in church when the worship leader is singing a song with believers all around you doing the same, it becomes very apparent that you aren't worshiping at home on a day-to-day basis either.

Let every moment, every action, every decision, and every step of your life be an expression of your love for him. Then, and only then, will you be able to make the most of your intimate times of prayer, Bible study, and participation in God's church. Worship is in the survival kit because it keeps every other part of the kit in proper balance. Without a heart of worship, Bible reading, prayer, and church attendance can still become meaningless.

WHAT'S NEXT?

This chapter also has an assignment. Without a decision, an action, and something in place to keep you accountable to that decision, it is highly unlikely that you will alter your current pattern of behavior. Don't forget to include your accountability partner in all of your lifestyle decisions.

1. Continue your intimate thirty-plus minutes of prayer and thirty-plus minutes of Scripture each day to keep your eyes fixed on Jesus. Without the gentle soaking rain of daily, habitual intimacy with God, you cannot truly worship him. And without worship, you cannot have meaningful, intimate time with him. Each needs the other.

2. Allow everything you do this week to become an expression of your love for Jesus, especially the challenging aspects. Your tense relationship with your boss, your meaningless tedium of daily household chores, and your frustration with your children are all your gift to God. Every moment is an opportunity to show God that he's calling the shots. If your obedience to your boss, your dirty dishes, and your children are all an expression of love, they will take on a whole new meaning.

3. Think of something in your life that has not yet been surrendered to Jesus and give it to him. Let the Holy Spirit speak. I think you'll know what you have to do. We all have something more that we're holding back from God. Maybe it's a comfortable sin you don't want to give up. Maybe you've been refusing to forgive someone. Maybe you just haven't allowed him to call the shots on an activity that's holding you back. I think you know the areas of your life you've been holding back. Make it an obedient sacrifice of worship and give it to Jesus once and for all. Live the rest of your life letting him be in charge of this one.

CHAPTER 5: WE NEED SHELTER

CHURCH

"The Lord God said, 'It is not good for the man to be alone. I will make a helper suitable for him'" (Genesis 2:18). Since the dawn of creation, we were not meant to work in isolation. Life is a group effort. Church is all about community. It's about loving people and being loved. It's about sharing what you gain here with those outside who need Jesus.

But before you start reading a chapter I've written on the subject, I have to confess to you that this is where I struggle the most. I was a pastor for thirteen years. I *attended* everything there was to attend, but being part of community in relationship with people in the church and using what I'd learned in church to relationally engage with unbelievers was a real challenge for me. But with the knowledge of its importance, and knowing that this is where I am weak, this where I spend the most effort in trying to grow. I just want you to know that we're all growing in all of these areas. Even the teacher can go deeper into the survival kit. The point is to recognize what was established in the first chapter of this book: there's always room for growth.

Now, let's quickly review the previous chapters:

1. You're already in a survival situation, so you need to continually prepare because you're never ready.
2. If you remain connected to Jesus, "The Vine," in prayer, you get the flow of his living water. Apart from him, you can do nothing.
3. Studying the instructions and training with your sword equips you for battle. Don't neglect the tools you've already been given.
4. Worship is the motivation for every spiritual discipline. If it's not done for God, why do it?
5. Everything you do can be done in worship to honor God.
6. Worship requires sacrifice.

I'm about to ask you some opening questions again. So, once again, be honest with yourself and think about what you really do from day to day. There's no reason to feel bad or good about your answers. This is just the starting point. Before you determine where you're going, you have to determine where you are.

1. Do you have to go to church to be a Christian?
2. What is the purpose of the church?

SECTION 1: THE NEED FOR SHELTER

A shelter can protect you from the sun, insects, wind, rain, snow, hot or cold temperatures, and enemy observation. A shelter can give you a feeling of well-being and help you maintain your will to survive.

I mentioned earlier that I've watched some extreme survivalist television shows. In one episode, some experts visited a family of doomsday preppers who wanted to be evaluated on their preparation in case society collapsed. They wanted to know if they had enough supplies and skills, as well as the means to protect what they had, should others wish to come and steal what they'd prepared.

The experts looked at their enormous property and tiny house and saw that there was no defendable position. They also looked at the mother and father and their six young children, all of who were far too young to pick up a weapon. If bandits from a collapsed society came storming up their front gates, this family would have had no way of stopping them. The expert evaluation was that they were well-supplied but unable to protect those supplies. The experts recommended that they build relationships and partnerships with their neighbors because there was no way they could protect their family of eight by themselves.

The couple disagreed and refused to even consider connecting with their neighbors. To prove their point, the experts gave the mother and father a pair of paintball guns and safety masks and held a mock attack. Four men pretended to be bandits, likewise using paintball guns, and challenged the couple to defend their home. The couple failed miserably.

After hearing the expert advice that they needed more help and should build relationships with their neighbors in case a disaster occurred, and after experiencing for themselves the truth of their inability to defend themselves alone, they *still* refused to consider including their neighbors in their preparation. They didn't want to depend on anyone else. The experts ended the evaluation shrugging their shoulders in disbelief that the family would refuse to simply connect with their neighbors, even after having seen for themselves that they wouldn't survive without others' help.

Community is shelter.

I've heard it said that you don't have to go to church to be a Christian. In a way that's true, but you also don't need water to be a fish. You're just not going to last very long. A fish out of water basically drowns in the air. It can't survive long out of water because it wasn't designed to live in that environment.

It's still a fish, but it's a sick and dying fish that won't last long on its own.

We were designed to live in community. It's repeated and demonstrated throughout Scripture. If you want to follow the technical manual, you don't have to go to church in order to accept salvation and forgiveness of sins. But the Christian life is more than just escaping hell. Do you want to be a Christian with abundant life or an unhealthy one prone to dying spiritually? You were meant to swim in a community. You don't have to go to church to be a saved, but you're not going to last long out of the water.

On the other hand, simply attending church doesn't make you a Christian any more than walking into a garage makes you a car. Being a teacher, deacon, or even pastor isn't what makes you a Christian either. We have to learn how to separate salvation from spiritual health. Salvation is about having your sins forgiven and restoring your relationship with God. That's a free gift paid for when Jesus died to take the punishment for your sins. But that is not where the journey ends. That's where the journey begins. Going to church isn't what you do to attain salvation. It's what saved people do to keep growing in this new, saved life they've been given.

When I was a young child, perhaps five years old, I watched a movie called *The Karate Kid*. After watching it, I was convinced I knew karate. I went up to my dad and told him that if a robber ever came into our house, I would beat him up with karate. Then I took my karate stance and put up my hands, slicing them in convincing little karate chops.

My dad didn't want his five-year-old believing he could challenge an adult stranger. So my dad did what any loving father should do. He put one finger on my forehead. In one push, he drove me straight to the ground. Then he said, "Philip, you don't know karate."

Of course, I ran off crying, but I learned a valuable lesson that day. Watching others do something doesn't mean I can do it too. Playing church doesn't mean you're a Christian, ready for the attacks life brings. One pastor at my church, Joel Slater, once said, "Time spent in church is not directly proportional to spiritual maturity." Isn't that the truth?

So if you can't survive without church, but going to church doesn't make you a good Christian, then what exactly is church?

SECTION 2: CHURCH IS NOT . . .

Before we can establish what church is, it's vital to establish what church is not. Children's ministry is easy because you have an empty slate where you can simply insert truth and the child can accept it. As adults, however, every truth we learn is filtered through a lifetime of experiences that have been lying to us for far too long. Sometimes we have to deprogram the mistakes so we can reprogram the truth. We wouldn't want any of the leftover lies to creep in and spoil any truth God pours in.

Here are a few misconceptions that some experiences may have led you to believe:

Church is not your primary source of spiritual growth (worship, prayer, Bible reading, etc.). The truth is, your personal time with God is your primary source of spiritual growth. Church is the supporting role, not the lead player. You are responsible for your own spiritual growth. Your actions cannot be dependent on others. You cannot control what others give or do not give you. The only thing you have control over is your choices. Do you choose to pursue God and grow or not?

Church is not your primary source of your connection with God. The truth is, *God* is your connection with God, not a person or establishment. You don't have to go through a priest to experience a connection with God. When Jesus died and rose from the dead, the curtain separating God's presence from the common people was torn in two. In other words, you don't have to wait for a pastor to pray for you. The same Holy Spirit Peter used to raise the dead in the Bible is the same Holy Spirit living in you.

Church is not your seclusion or isolation from the world. The truth is, church is where you go to equip yourself to *engage* your world. You don't hunker down in the church like it's some sort of bomb shelter waiting for the world to pass by. There's a world of lost, hurting, and dying souls out there that our Savior commanded us to reach. He saved you not so you could isolate yourself, but so you could go out and share that salvation with others. If you're going to church to shut out the world, you're missing the point.

Church is not a mere social club. The truth is, if you wanted a social club you could join the YMCA or the Lions Club. If all you want is a place to belong and make a positive difference, you don't need the church. You don't even need God for that. If your engagement with your church doesn't contain something life-changing and world-shaking, then you might be treating it like a social club.

Church is not where you hide your flaws to avoid judgment. The truth is, we were commanded to confess our sins to one another to be healed and encouraged (James 5). We're all in this fight together. There are countless pretty people wearing whitewashed masks to church so no one will find out that they have problems. That's how the enemy can keep breeding those flaws in people's lives. Anything that stays secret stays untreated. If the enemy can get you to hide your hardships, you'll never be able to get the encouragement and support to overcome them. Many Christians who seem perfect on the outside are just waiting for someone to be courageous enough to be vulnerable so they can confess their weaknesses to someone who understands.

Church is not perfection. The truth is, we're still a gathering of imperfect, broken people. To expect anything else is unrealistic. Take no offense. Expect mistakes. Not every decision the pastor makes will lead to your definition of success. Some people are still struggling with their temptation to gossip. When someone says or does something that hurts your feelings, remember that you're not perfect either, and the church let you through the front doors too. We're all figuring this stuff out a day at a time, and we have to learn to love and encourage one another through our flaws.

SECTION 3: CHURCH IS . . .

Now we come to the crux of the matter. If you want to know what the shelter of the church really is, you have to look away from your own experiences. You have to look away from what others have told you church is. You have to look away from examples you've observed. You have to go back to the source: the inescapable truth of God's Word.

Church is your shelter and safe place to be vulnerable. James 5:16 says, "Therefore confess your sins to each other and pray for each other so that you may be healed. The prayer of a righteous person is powerful and effective." Ephesians 5:11 says, "Have nothing to do with the fruitless deeds of darkness, but rather expose them."

Church is your encouragement. Hebrews 10:24–25 says, "And let us consider how we may spur one another on toward love and good deeds, not giving up meeting together, as some are in the habit of doing, but encouraging one another—and all the more as you see the Day approaching."

Church is where you learn how to connect with God at home. Philippians 4:9 says, "Whatever you have learned or received or heard from me, or seen in me—put it into practice. And the God of peace will be with you."

Church is a place for discipleship (both to you and by you). Matthew 28:18–19 says, "Then Jesus came to them and said, 'All authority in heaven and on earth has been given to me. Therefore go and make disciples of all nations, baptizing them in the name of the Father and of the Son and of the Holy Spirit.'" Furthermore, the apostle Paul had mentors, peers and disciples. It would benefit us to live after his example. We all need someone who has walked before us to show us the way, someone to walk with us to pick us up when we stumble, and someone to follow in our footsteps as we pass on what we learn. Consider Paul's words in 1 Corinthians 4:17: "For this reason I have sent to you Timothy, my son whom I love, who is faithful in the Lord. He will remind you of my way of life in Christ Jesus, which agrees with what I teach everywhere in every church."

Church is your training ground for leading the unsaved to Christ. Ephesians 3:10 says, "His intent was that now, through the church, the manifold wisdom of God should be made known to the rulers and authorities in the heavenly realms." It is *not* the job of the corporate organization of the church to win the lost so we don't have to. It's your job as *part* of the church. It's not the pastor's job as a minister to win the lost. It's his job as a believer. His job as pastor is to equip you to win the lost. People rarely get saved through a VBS or a Christmas Concert. They get saved through a *relationship* with a Christian like you. Church is the training ground. Paul spoke about this at length in Ephesians 4:11–16:

> So Christ himself gave the apostles, the prophets, the evangelists, the pastors and teachers, *to equip his people for works of service,* so that the body of Christ may be built up until we all reach unity in the faith and in the knowledge of the Son of

God and become mature, attaining to the whole measure of the fullness of Christ.

Then we will no longer be infants, tossed back and forth by the waves, and blown here and there by every wind of teaching and by the cunning and craftiness of people in their deceitful scheming. Instead, *speaking the truth* in love, we will grow to become in every respect the mature body of him who is the head, that is, Christ. From him the whole body, joined and held together by every supporting ligament, grows and *builds itself up* in love, as each part *does its work* (Emphasis added).

Church is your accountability to spiritual discipline, morality, and correct understanding. In Matthew 8:15–17, Jesus said, "If your brother or sister sins, go and point out their fault, just between the two of you. If they listen to you, you have won them over. But if they will not listen, take one or two others along, so that 'every matter may be established by the testimony of two or three witnesses.' If they still refuse to listen, tell it to the church; and if they refuse to listen even to the church, treat them as you would a pagan or a tax collector." Others can see your errors before you can. We need others to point out if we seem to be straying off the path. We also need to love others enough to let them know if we see them about to crash and burn. If someone can't listen to advice from fellow believers, then they should be treated like a pagan. In other words, they need to be loved back into being saved.

Church is your place to serve fellow believers and contribute to all of the above. Again, Paul had much to write about this:

> Just as a body, though one, has many parts, but all its many parts form one body, so it is with Christ. For we were all baptized by one Spirit so as to form one body—whether Jews or Gentiles, slave or free—and we were all given the one Spirit to drink. Even so the body is not made up of one part but of many.
>
> Now if the foot should say, "Because I am not a hand, I do not belong to the body," it would not for that reason stop being part of the body. And if the ear should say, "Because I am not an eye, I do not belong to the body," it would not for that reason stop being part of the body. If the whole body were an eye, where would the sense of hearing be? If

> the whole body were an ear, where would the sense of smell be? But in fact God has placed the parts in the body, every one of them, just as he wanted them to be. If they were all one part, where would the body be?
>
> As it is, there are many parts, but one body. . . . Now you are the body of Christ, and each one of you is a part of it (1 Corinthians 12:12–20, 27).

We all have a part to play, and no one part is more important than another. Worship leaders are not more important than nursery workers. Whatever your role, you are an active part of what God wants to do through the church. You are the recipient of much. Now share what you have received and help others be vulnerable, receive encouragement, connect with God, get discipled, learn how to share Jesus, and submit to accountability. Freely you have received, freely give.

People try to argue that they can be a Christian without going to church, or that they don't need the church. But based on the truth of God's Word they're wrong. These are only a few of the supporting scriptures. What they should say is that they don't need the church to be saved, because salvation is an act of God in the heart. Christianity is a community of people. To isolate oneself is not only self-destructive, it's selfish.

They neglect to realize that the church needs them too. They mistakenly believe that the church exists only to serve them. They forget that they are there to serve the church too.

SECTION 4: BUT . . .

I know that when some read a description of how they're supposed to get involved in church, they instantly recoil from it by citing the hurt that church has inflicted on them. How can someone be expected to be vulnerable when they laid their soul bare at church and got wounded for their trouble? How can someone be expected to seek discipleship from leaders that live in failure? How can someone be expected to seek encouragement when all they've received in church is criticism?

My response to questions like that is, "That's *not* God's church!"

I once walked into a filthy fast food restaurant that was full of rude employees. Does that mean all restaurants are rude and dirty and should be avoided? Of course not. That's absurd. That restaurant was not functioning the way it was supposed to. You cannot judge God's church based on your hurts.

The reason you find pain, hypocrisy, and hate in churches is because there are individuals in these churches who are not functioning in obedience to God's Word. They are not properly connected to him in prayer. They are not active in worship. They've lost their survival kits. They're dying. Some church communities have the maturity to correct these lost individuals. Some do not. But in either case, don't throw the baby out with the bathwater. Just because a group of broken individuals did you wrong under the disguise of church life doesn't mean you can discount the entire church altogether.

Ray Noah, my pastor, put it this way: "The church is God's plan to save the world and there is no Plan B." In other words, God established us as his church and told us to save the world. God gave us the instructions on how we are to run his church. It's our responsibility to do everything we can as individuals to be the church he described. The more Christians who get on board with that, the closer the church will resemble God's perfect plan. It's not your responsibility to fix the church or rebuke the church. It's your job to *be* the church.

At this point I know what some people might be tempted to think: the obvious solution is to simply leave the church that hurt you and find a better one. Well, I admit, sometimes there are rare examples where a church is so far away from God and in such dramatic error that it would be dangerous to stay in that environment, but cases like that are actually very rare. If you pick up and move out when you face toxic relationships or get wounded by people, you will never land anywhere. It is nearly impossible to find an environment free from pain. And, chances are, when someone moves to a new church they'll take their hurt with them, and even the new church can't stand a chance because, at the first sign of struggle, the relocated Christian will write it off as, "Just another church that's going to let me down again."

When Jesus's disciples made stupid mistakes, asked stupid questions, criticized his choices, or started bickering amongst themselves, did he throw them out and get newer, better disciples? No. He invested deeper into their growth. When the apostle Paul heard that the church in Corinth was falling apart with false doctrine and social chaos, did he abandon them? No. He sent more people to get more involved. He sent Timothy. He wanted to go back and visit himself. He recommended that his friend Apollos pay them a visit. He wrote to them, encouraging and correcting them. He prayed for them constantly. He didn't jump ship and swim away. He invested deeper into their maturity.

The solution is rarely to leave the church. The solution is to invest deeper into making it better. We don't make it better by rebelling against what the leadership is doing or causing division by getting people on our side or stirring up arguments. We make it better by doing as Matthew 5:16 commands: "In the same way, let your light shine before others, that they may see your good deeds and glorify your Father in heaven."

SECTION 5: PRACTICALITY

All of the above sections are great information philosophically, but now that we know what the church is supposed to be, what do we do with that information? Does this just mean we have to go to church more? No. Just like prayer, Bible reading, and worship, participating in church needs to be a part of who we are, not just something we do. Church is not a religious requirement or some ceremonial routine. It's about making the community of your fellow believers a higher priority in life.

Church is people. Programs, sermons, music, and activities are things that happen within the community of people. But the church itself is people. Before you're tempted to develop a problem with any program, sermon, or activity, remember: it's not about those things. It's about people. We can't connect with God spiritually unless we connect with each other relationally. It's been true since the Garden of Eden.

Church (along with Bible reading and prayer) takes a higher seat in your life than work, school, and recreation. That may rub some of you the wrong way. We're taught in our culture to prioritize work and education over everything else. But these things do not benefit your eternal condition. They just affect your temporary condition on earth.

Prioritizing church is lived out in your choices. When church competes with something else, which one wins? Don't take a job if it requires you to work on Sundays. Or quit. Yes, I said quit. My family had to quit a job because it was spiritually harmful and we really couldn't afford to quit at the time. If soccer practice competes with church, go to church and either skip practice or find a sport that practices on Tuesdays. If you need to drop six credits at school so you can volunteer in the church nursery, make it happen.

What affects the eternal is always more important than what affects the temporary. Remember the string from the last chapter? Why prioritize a job, degree, or hobby when everything they produce is going to wither and burn? Invest in spiritual disciplines and don't compromise them. When you put the things of God first, as the foundation you cannot compromise, something supernatural happens in the spiritual realm. God releases his favor and allows you the time for everything else you need (Matthew 6:33).

We often have the opportunity to pursue things that conflict with church, such as a sport or recreational activity that practices on Sundays. Think about your kids' soccer team and compare it to something else they could pursue, such as Junior Bible Quiz, Awana clubs, or a Sunday School program. You could argue some benefit for soccer, such as teamwork or exercise. But isn't their eternal spiritual condition so much more important than that? Wouldn't something like an Awana club give them scriptural tools to benefit both their life on earth and their eternity? When they're forty and have kids of their own, don't you want them to care about the eternal spiritual condition of your grandkids, or would you rather they teach your grandkids that trivial pursuits take priority over the King of the universe who died for them?

I am *not* saying that you can't go to a soccer game or a business trip if it lands on a Sunday. There are exceptions when, once in a while, something important does prevent you from going to church. When my kids had a school play on the same day as the church choir rehearsal, we talked it over as a family and were perfectly willing to skip that rehearsal to attend our kids' play. When we recently took our summer vacation, we didn't go to church that Sunday. We went to Disneyland. But this is not our regular practice. In life and in general, we don't allow ourselves to place any regular pursuit above our commitment to attend church.

Serve! Church is not a spectator sport. It's a team sport. It's a community, not a concert. We don't come only to receive. We come to contribute too. Explore your abilities and seek out how you can use them to help the church achieve its mission. Study your gifts and talents and find the areas where you can serve with those gifts.

Use and apply what you learn in church to your daily life. Take your pastor's challenges seriously. Invite friends to church events. Share with your friends the life and encouragement you get from the community of Christ. Let the things you learn there fuel your daily pursuit of Christ. After all, if you're not applying what you hear in the sermons, why are you listening to them?

SECTION 6: MY EXPERIENCE

I've lived at church all my life, from attending everything as a pastor's kid to attending everything as a pastor. But as both the child of a pastor and later as a pastor myself, I faced a unique challenge. Was I serving because it was what my family did? Was I serving because it was my job? When my occupation was to serve others, it was really hard to tell if it was an act of love and worship or if I was just getting paid to do it.

When I chose to resign as a pastor to pursue my writing and resourcing career, I was actually pretty scared. I was afraid that I was only involved in church because I was required to be. I was afraid that I was only connecting with people because it was part of my job. If I was no longer employed by the church, would

I even want to continue serving? Would I want to get up on a Sunday morning to attend if I didn't have any responsibilities? If I weren't a pastor, would I really want to serve as a volunteer?

As it turns out, I was worried for nothing.

I connected with people just as easily, if not easier, when I was no longer a pastor. I served with more focus and more passion as a volunteer than I had as an employee. I finally saw that I was truly interested in serving people and not because it was my job. I *wanted* to be at church. The reason I lived at church was not because my dad worked there or because I worked there. It was because the church was my home. The church was where the presence of God, lived out in a community, could support me. The church was where I felt I had something useful and meaningful to contribute. Once I realized this, church became more personally fulfilling. Investing in that community *outside* of any occupational requirement became one of the most beautifully satisfying experiences of my life.

On a not-too-serious note, my only challenge now is that I am no longer in the church office or staff meetings to learn about church events. I actually have to pay attention to bulletins and announcement emails like a civilian. Oh well.

WHAT'S NEXT?

I'm sure it comes as no surprise that this chapter also has an assignment. Without a decision, an action, and something in place to keep you accountable to that decision, it is highly unlikely that you will alter your current patterns of behavior. Don't forget to include your accountability partner in all of your lifestyle decisions.

1. Continue your intimate thirty-plus minutes of prayer and thirty-plus minutes of Scripture reading each day to keep your eyes fixed on Jesus. Remember, church is not the source of your relationship with God. That's between you and God. Church supports that relationship. It's still your responsibility to personally pursue Christ.

2. Evaluate if there are other temporal pursuits that are taking priority over your eternal spiritual pursuits in church. Do you participate in a church community every week? Is there anything standing in the way of you becoming involved more than once a week? Take eternity seriously. It's time to start shifting where you spend your time. When church conflicts with something else, let church win.

3. If you haven't yet found a place to serve in your church, explore what area you can serve starting this week. You know there's probably an announcement in the weekly bulletin or an event coming up that's asking for volunteers to serve: pick up trash, mow the lawns, hold babies in the nursery, teach a Sunday School class. They've been waiting and praying for someone to raise their hand and step up. Be that person. Talk to your church leader before Sunday.

CHAPTER 6: MAKE IT REAL

You can do this. Survival preparation is nothing more than making sure that the perishable supplies in your kit get refreshed as often as they need to. There is no challenge you cannot overcome. There is no problem you cannot survive. There is no vision you cannot achieve when you live these essentials for life on a regular basis. But beware: compromise one and the others cannot work right.

Prayer. Connecting daily and intimately with God in prayer is your number one priority in life. Without prayer, Bible reading is nothing more than information transfer and can never affect you personally. Without prayer, worship is nothing more than lip service and emotional placebos. Without prayer, church is a social club where you learn about God but never meet him for yourself. You need prayer.

Bible study. Receiving the daily bread of God's truth becomes your weapon, your guide, and your light. Without Bible study, prayer can be misguided. Without Bible study, your worship may be far from the worship God desires. Without Bible study, you won't be able to weigh and measure what you're taught in church against the truth of God's Word. You need Bible study.

Worship. Worship is the fuel that motivates all of your spiritual pursuits and keeps everything in balance. Without worship, prayer becomes mechanical. Without worship, Bible study becomes a book report. Without worship, what you do in church is self-serving instead of God-glorifying. You need worship.

Church. Church is your support community that keeps encouraging you toward a deeper pursuit of Christ and his mission. Without church, prayer can never achieve the power of praying together, praying with others, or receiving prayer from others. Without church, Bible study can easily stray into misunderstanding because of a lack of guidance. Without church, worship cannot be enjoyed together as a community the way God demonstrated and instructed in the Bible. You need church.

Begin sowing these seeds. "Do not be deceived: God cannot be mocked. A man reaps what he sows. Whoever sows to please their flesh, from the flesh will reap destruction; whoever sows to please the Spirit, from the Spirit will reap eternal life. Let us not become weary in doing good, for at the proper time we will reap a harvest if we do not give up. Therefore, as we have opportunity, let us do good to all people, especially to those who belong to the family of believers" (Galatians 6:7–10).

What must you do to be a disciple?

> From that time on Jesus began to explain to his disciples that he must go to Jerusalem and suffer many things at the hands of the elders, the chief priests and the teachers of the law, and that he must be killed and on the third day be raised to life.
>
> Peter took him aside and began to rebuke him. "Never, Lord!" he said. "This shall never happen to you!"
>
> Jesus turned and said to Peter, "Get behind me, Satan! You are a stumbling block to me; you do not have in mind the concerns of God, but merely human concerns."
>
> Then Jesus said to his disciples, "Whoever wants to be my disciple must deny themselves and take up their cross and follow me. For whoever wants to save their life will lose it, but whoever loses their life for me will find it. What good will it be for someone to gain the whole world, yet forfeit their soul? Or what can anyone give in exchange for their soul? For the Son of Man is going to come in

> his Father's glory with his angels, and then he will reward each person according to what they have done (Matthew 16:21–27).

Remember not to get discouraged. Failure is your best teacher. Success is your best encourager.

The good habits I've shared in this book take time to develop. Don't quit. You can do it. Keep trying day-by-day, and in a few weeks you will notice a good routine forming and you will see your hard work pay off.

I pray that this survival kit motivates you to deeply pursue your personal, intimate relationship with Jesus every day for the rest of your life. I hope that out of a true desire to know God and his perfect purpose for your life, you will long for and chase after him with a heart of worship in intimate prayer and meaningful Bible study, with the support and guidance of your church community. Then, when your basic spiritual needs are being met, you will have access to all the blessings and growth that come from a healthy, foundational, and active relationship with Jesus.

**Philip Hahn** is a second-generation children's pastor with a BA in Children's Ministries from North Central University. Philip has been a children's pastor, TV host, camp director, as well as the speaker at many special events, conferences, and camps. He has experience speaking to kids, teens, and adults in everything from classrooms to auditoriums. Philip believes there is no Biblical truth too complicated to teach to a child if it is taught in a simple way. This philosophy makes his teaching simple to understand and easy to apply to all ages. He is married to his best friend Chanda and they reside in Portland, Oregon with their twin children.

For information on SourceBox Production's *Illuminate Curriculum* or to contact the author concerning speaking engagements, please visit:

www.sourceboxproductions.com

www.ingramcontent.com/pod-product-compliance
Lightning Source LLC
Chambersburg PA
CBHW060016050426
42448CB00012B/2781